JanBraai

BRAAIBROODJIES AND BURGERS

This book is dedicated to the millions of South Africans who celebrate National Braai Day on 24 September every year.

In National Braai Day, we South Africans have a realistic opportunity to entrench and cement a national day of celebration for our country, within our lifetimes. I believe that having a national day of celebration can play a significant role in nation-building and social cohesion as the observance of our shared heritage can truly bind us together.

In Africa, a fire is the traditional place of gathering. I urge you to get together with your friends and family around a fire on 24 September every year to celebrate our heritage, share stories and pass on traditions. Please help me spread that word!

JanBraai

BRAAIBROODJIES AND BURGERS

BOOK**STORM**

CONTENTS

INTRODUCTION 9
The best bread for a braaibroodjie 10
Cutting of corners 12
History of the hamburger 12
My (current) view on hamburger patties 14
The best roll for a hamburger 16
How to braai chicken breast fillets as burger patties 17

BRAAIBROODJIES 18
Traditional braaibroodjie 20
Biltong braaibroodjie 22
The Supermodel 24
Chorizo braaibroodjie 26
Bacon and banana braaibroodjie 29
Spanakopita braaibroodjie 30
Breakfast braaibroodjie 32
Curry mince braaibroodjie 34
Greek-style braaibroodjie 36
Holy Trinity braaibroodjie 39
Break-time braaibroodjie 41
Three-cheese braaibroodjie 43
West Coast braaibroodjie 44
Club braaibroodjie 46
Peri-peri chicken liver braaibroodjie 48
Cheese and herb braaibroodjie 50

Chicken mayo braaibroodjie 52
Mushroom braaibroodjie 55
Empanada braaibroodjie 56
Deluxe braaibroodjie 58
Fig and feta braaibroodjie 60
Calamari braaibroodjie 62
Anchovy, caper and olive braaibroodjie 64
Snoek braaibroodjie 67
Braaied butternut braaibroodjie 68
Raclette braaibroodjie 70
Macaroni and cheese braaibroodjie 72
Bagel braaibroodjie 74
The burger braaibroodjie 76
Jan Braai lamb pita 78
Bolognese quesadillas 80
Jan Braai pizza 83
The iced-tea sandwich 84
Caramel braaibroodjie 87
Classic scone braaibroodjie 88
Chocolate braaibroodjie 90
Waffle braaibroodjie 92
Apple tart braaibroodjie 94
Marshmallow and chocolate braaibroodjie 96

BURGERS	100
The best amazing mushroom burger	103
Caprese burger	104
Monkeygland burger	107
Fillet and bone marrow burger	108
Bobotie burger	110
Madagascan peppercorn burger	112
Nacho burger	114
Steak prego roll	117
The Big burger	118
Cheese and bacon burger	120
The stout beer burger	122
Steak sandwich with mustard, mayo and caramelised onions	124
Hand-chopped burger	127
Mustard and caper burger	128
Braai Freedom Fighter	130
Chimichurri steak roll	133
Bacon, pineapple and sweet-chilli burger	134
The Bash burger	136
Irish Wild West Coast burger	138
Rogan Josh burger	141
The Garlic burger	142
Chakalaka burger	145
Burgundy burger	146
Spiced bacon and cheese burger	148
Sloppy Jan	150
Lamb burger	152
Pork neck burger	154
Pork belly burger	156
Choripán burger	159
Pulled pork party	160
Sherry boerewors sliders	162
Klein Karoo ostrich burger	164
The Revolutionary mushroom burger	166
Teriyaki tuna burger	168
Fish cake burger	171
Cape Malay fish burger	172
How to make potato wedges	174
Roosterkoek	176
Chicken prego roll	178
Crispy chicken burger	180
Chicken, Camembert, fig and bacon burger	182
The Rotherhamburger	184
The Mule	186
SMOG burger	188
Chicken, feta and sun-dried tomato burger	190
Blue cheese burger	192
Klein Karoo chicken burger	194
Chicken Caesar burger	196
INDEX	200

INTRODUCTION

Fun is the single word that describes this book best. A braaibroodjie is your chance in life to have the bread buttered on both sides, literally. And packing that bread with delicious fillings before toasting it over the coals of a wooden fire is just the way to celebrate life, considering you only live once. On that note, you might as well then go full throttle with this one life because the book you are holding not only has a selection of real masterpiece braaibroodjies, but also an arsenal of burgers that epitomise the concept of hitting the ball out of the park when cooking great food on a fire.

Fundamentally, braaibroodjies and burgers are fun items at the fire. These are straightforward ingredients that you can find in any supermarket; quick to prepare, meaning that you can start by lighting the fire and easily do all the other work by the time your coals are ready; and easy to braai (it's not a thick cut of meat that needs you to do aerial acrobatics above the fire for hours before it's cooked on the inside without the outsides burning, nor is it a tough cut of meat that need to become tender in a potjie before the rest of the ingredients and the world turns into soup). With braaibroodjies, the actual braai part only has one trick: turn as often as possible. With burger patties, the trick is the exact opposite: only turn once. These techniques are discussed in detail in all relevant recipes, so I am convinced you will not struggle.

As all the wonderful photos in this book attest to, braaibroodjies and burgers are pleasing to the eye and very photogenic. Braaibroodjies and burgers are also easy to eat. They make for straightforward guest and table management as they are consumed in total, with no leftover skin, bones or shells. More often than not, cutlery isn't even necessary, and after the feast, there are just empty plates.

Creating this book was a whole lot of fun and I hope and trust that you will find the same amount of joy using it. Using the book to page through should be fun, preparing the recipes in this book should be fun, and eating the braaibroodjies and burgers you make from this book really should be fun.

Publishing a book solely dedicated to these two fun stars of the braai fire has been a long-term goal of mine and I am delighted to finally present you with the finished product. The advantage of taking so many years to reach this point is that by now, I am surrounded by a very strong support team in a project like this, without whom the work of art in your hands would simply not be such a wonderful work of art.

At the time of first publishing this book, the year 2020, social media is the way in which all of us humans communicate and stay in touch. When you're having as much fun using this book as we had creating it, please share that fun with me. On all major social media platforms, I can be found on @janbraai and let's all use the hashtag #braaibroodjiesandburgers when talking about the fun we're having! I look forward to sitting at my braai fire and seeing photos of your braaibroodjies and burgers at your braai fire. Thank you for the support in buying this book and please continue helping me to spread the message of uniting this nation around a fire!

Most importantly, have fun.

Jan Braai

The best bread for a braaibroodjie

The braaibroodjie is not simply the best thing since sliced bread – it's better than sliced bread and coincidentally, a consequence of sliced bread. There are rare exceptions for some of the more exotic variations of braaibroodjie in this book but a braaibroodjie is almost exclusively best made by using plain, straightforward white sliced bread.

When I was a kid, these breads were sold as a single unit and either in the bakery area of the supermarket or close to the payment points, the store would have a machine for you to slice your own bread. These machines sliced the whole loaf in uniform slices and the slices were also typically thinner than if you sliced that same bread with a bread knife at home.

Nowadays, most supermarkets sell a few commercial brands of white sliced bread. And that is what I almost always buy to make braaibroodjies. I say 'almost always' because sometimes that is not available in a supermarket and on those rare occasions, not by choice but by force, I buy something else.

My knowledge of sliced white bread does not extend to having any idea why some commercial bread suppliers make an oversized version but frankly, there is no justification for that, nor any place for it in the making of braaibroodjies. These oversized slices do not hold up when building the braaibroodjies, nor when moving the braaibroodjies from your chopping board or similar vehicle of preparation to the braai grid. Due to their non-perfect outline, they also do not pack as neatly into a braai grid and thus, should be avoided.

Commercial bread suppliers also sell to supermarkets a sliced bread similar in shape and size to the real plain, straightforward white sliced bread – only it's not entirely white and it's polluted with bits of bran. Very optimistically, they call this 'brown bread', which it certainly is not. More accurately, it's off-white with speckles. I frankly find it disgusting. I can only hazard a guess that this is a misguided attempt to make it more healthy but there's a look, flavour and texture that I find unappetising, to put it more mildly.

I am no dietician and there is no medical basis for anything I say, but I do believe that if sacrificing braaibroodjies made with perfectly beautiful white sliced bread for this so-called 'brown bread' version is your last hope at getting enough roughage into your digestive system, then you are beyond salvation anyway. Eat your fruit and vegetables in their natural state like you should, and enjoy your braaibroodjies properly – made with sliced white bread.

For the record, I have no problem with actual wholewheat and other breads with more personality, inherent taste and darker colours. I really enjoy proper bread from shades of caramel or brown like sourdough all the way to German Schwarzbrot. Just not for a braaibroodjie.

Of course, we're generalising here and in an emergency, absolutely any bread will work for a braaibroodjie because obviously any braaibroodjie is better than no braaibroodjie.

A last word of bread advice, entirely non-scientific, with no basis in fact and purely from personal observation: sliced white bread loaves usually contain at least 20 slices of usable bread and the least I have ever counted was 18. This means that I've yet to encounter a normal supermarket pre-packed sliced white bread loaf that cannot make at least nine braaibroodjies. Most can make 10.

Cutting of corners

As you all know (or should know) or will know after reading the very first braaibroodjie recipe in this book, the traditional recipe is to butter the bread on the outside and have a filling of cheese, tomato, onion, salt, pepper and chutney. Any deviation from this is exactly that – a deviation.

The widely accepted way to mark a non-regulation braaibroodjie is to cut a corner off that one, so as to distinguish it from all the others. You are not cutting the corner of the non-regulation braaibroodjie to victimise the eater thereof, but to protect them from mistakenly eating the wrong braaibroodjie and exposing their delicate digestive or emotional system to something it cannot tolerate.

There are some special-needs people in the world – not in the medical sense, but in the sense that there are people who consider their needs special, who find themselves unable to eat a braaibroodjie as it was originally intended. Typical examples of these unique characters might be people who request that their braaibroodjie is constructed without the use of chutney, or by omitting the tomato or the onion, or any other similar ridiculous request their mothers most likely taught them is acceptable to make.

Everything I say here, and also in the rest of the book, should be taken with a bit of braai salt. In that light-hearted context, I would like to tell you, special snowflake with your cut corner braaibroodjie, that this practice is not just to help you identify your 'safe' meal. It's actually your mark of shame. For being full of it.

And on an equally serious note, the South African braai is more than just the preparation of food. It's an ancient social ritual of togetherness – where people meet and socialise and exchange thoughts. When and if you are in the age bracket or stage of your life when you might be on the lookout for a life partner, a social braai is also a great place for such endeavours. It's relaxed and informal and although not everyone knows each other, everybody probably knows somebody and thus, in a wider sense, every person comes vetted to a better degree than a completely random stranger on the street. Beware of the individual eating the braaibroodjie with cut corners.

Such individuals (I'm generalising here) are what could be described as higher maintenance. Committing to any sort of relationship with this person is most likely to be more troublesome than a partnership with a similarly suitable individual who eats a braaibroodjie as is.

History of the hamburger

Here follows a simplified tale of the hamburger as I know it.

The story begins in the early 1200s with Mongolian warrior Genghis Khan and his troops riding around on horses and pretty much taking over the world. They would place pieces of meat between the saddle and the horse, leave the meat there until tenderised and then eat that as a snack on the go. I've read a few books on Genghis and this method of meat-eating pales in comparison with some of the things they did in battle, so you can relax.

A generation later, Kublai Khan, grandson of Genghis, invaded Russia and settled down in Moscow. The Russians then also started to eat tenderised meat, but thought of adding spices. They called it 'steak tartare' – Tartars being their name for some of the Mongolian warriors. Today, a modern version of steak tartare is still on many menus around the world.

During the 1500s and 1600s, Hamburg developed into the seaport hub of Europe, similar to De Aar being South Africa's train travel hub during the 1900s. Naturally, the steak tartare trend passed through and was adopted there.

This ball of spiced minced meat (which today we call a patty or meatball) was loved by American and German sailors, who took the meal to America, and specifically the port of New York. Here, it was not only served raw, but also cooked, and called a 'Hamburger steak' after the post where the recipe came from.

History is unclear on exactly what happened next, but somewhere between 1880 and 1900, some Americans had the idea of serving the hamburger steak between two pieces of bread. Originally called the 'Hamburger steak sandwich', it later evolved to just being called the hamburger.

My (current) view on hamburger patties

When you decide to braai hamburgers, you've got a few options as far as the patties go. In diminishing order of importance and eating pleasure they include:

- Homemade patties with hand-chopped mince
- Homemade patties with mince from your own mincer at home
- Homemade patties with mince freshly minced in front of your eyes at a butchery (this can be a supermarket or independent butchery)
- Homemade patties with mince bought at the supermarket
- Quality store-bought patties
- Below-par store-bought patties

Whichever route you decide to follow on any particular day usually depends on how much time you have at your disposal, how much effort you're willing to put in, and how big your craving is for a truly memorable work-of-art burger.

With 500 g of pure-beef mince, I think you can make four very decent hamburger patties of 125 g each and that is what I suggest you do for most beef burger recipes in this book – be that mince you produce at home, mince you get at a butchery, or mince you buy at a supermarket.

When mincing at home, you will need to start with slightly more than 500 g of meat to end with that, as a bit of sinew and the like will be filtered out by the mincer. Also take into account whether the meat you buy contains bones as is usually the case with, for example, chuck.

When making hamburger patty mince, I think best practice is to go for a rough split of half hindquarter meat (as it is more tender and has less fat) and the other half forequarter meat (which has more flavour and more fat). In practical terms, this usually means sirloin or rump steak from the hindquarter for me. Topside and silverside work equally well but are usually not sold in such small portions in supermarkets. For the other half of the meat, from the more flavourful forequarter, it's usually chuck for me. Any one or a combination of rib-eye, prime rib, chuck or brisket works – but to make a hassle-free trip to a single supermarket where you can buy all the ingredients for a burger recipe in this book, I'm happy to buy off-the-shelf, grab-and-go portions of sirloin or rump, and chuck.

When converting steak into mince with a mincer or chopping it by hand, you want the meat as cold as possible, so cut the steak into thin strips or small cubes, put them in a bowl and place in your freezer for an hour or two before you start.

The choice between mincing and hand-chopping usually comes down to whether you own a mincer. Mincing makes the job easier but means more dishwashing, and hand-chopping is more work but means only a knife and chopping board need to be washed. Hand-chopping a steak into mince doesn't really need to be an overly aggressive process involving a large cleaver, as a solid and sharp chef's knife will do the trick. For a detailed description on how to produce a hand-chopped burger, follow the Hand-Chopped Burger recipe on page 127.

Your own recently washed hands are entirely capable of forming patties from mince but I suggest you invest in a patty press or patty mould. These gadgets make it easy to form consistently sized and shaped patties. They have no electronics in them (so they don't really break), are about the size of a hamburger (so store easily) and cost about the price of a kilogram of fillet steak. Perfect to give or receive as a birthday gift. That is of course if you and everyone you know already owns this book, which is obviously an even better present.

To my mind, you should not add any spices, not even salt, to the mince. You're eating 100% pure steak, after all – you've just rearranged its shape. The fat strips have been minced or chopped up and spread evenly inside the meat; there are no tough bits in the steak and it has a uniform shape, which will braai more evenly. That's also why I believe you should braai a homemade burger patty medium rare, exactly like a steak. When compressed into nice round and flat patty shapes (with your patty press or cold, wet, recently washed hands), 100% pure beef patties do not fall apart when braaied, if you handle them with care. There is really no need for egg, breadcrumbs or any other binding agent.

At the time of writing this book, there was a move by some supermarkets to start selling high-quality fresh hamburger patties with few or no ingredients but pure beef. Hopefully, the increased demand for high-quality

pure-beef hamburger patties this book should generate will see an increased retail focus on providing us braai-loving public with these products.

You braai a homemade burger patty on an open grid over very high heat. The high heat sears and seals the meat, and makes the surface of the patty firm before it has the chance to 'sink' into the grid and get stuck. Although the patty will hold its form without any binding agents, don't tempt fate or test this principle to its limit. Only turn the patty once, as you would do with that same steak in its original shape. A steak takes about 8 minutes on very high heat to become medium rare, and so does this patty. Leave it for 4 minutes, carefully turn it over, then braai for 4 minutes on the other side.

The only condiment that you need to add to the patties while they are braaing is pure sea salt. You can add all the other flavours in the form of sauce or burger toppings afterwards.

The best roll for a hamburger

The best bread roll to use for a hamburger is the one you don't notice when enjoying said burger. Too substantial a roll and you're eating a piece of bread that happens to contain fillings or toppings. Such a meal is called a sandwich. With not enough body and substance to the roll to carry the patty, other toppings and sauces will make you aware of the bread roll (or rather, the absence thereof). Such a meal is called a mess.

The best roll for a specific burger will not be the same roll for all burgers and will depend on the other contents, so choose wisely and more importantly, with common sense. For meals like the Braai Freedom Fighter (page 130), for example, you will choose a more solid hamburger bread roll and in the case of wonderful recipes like the Monkeygland Burger (page 107) and the Revolutionary Mushroom Burger (page 166), you preferably want the freshest, but most inconsequential supermarket roll you can find – barely more than an edible sauce-absorbing serviette to hold the patty.

Delving into the finer details, in most cases, hamburger rolls will be slightly more stable if you slice them open with a sharp, ragged-tooth bread knife,

maintaining their structural integrity (as opposed to simply breaking them open). Buttering the insides of the rolls gives them a layer, a slight additional barrier of protection from sauces (be that the juices of the braaied patty or the actual sauce you're adding to the burger) seeping into the rolls and making them disintegrate. Best practice is to spread the sliced rolls on the inside with butter or olive oil and then toast them on a grid over the coals for the last few minutes of the braai and in most burger recipes in this book, that is what I suggest you do. It helps the roll hold its shape but more importantly, makes it taste even better.

Irrespective of absolutely anything, you can always serve any braaied burger with freshly baked roosterkoek (page 176) off the fire. Barring roosterkoek, remember the golden rule: the best roll for the hamburger is the one you didn't notice was there or not there.

How to braai chicken breast fillets as burger patties

Of the big four of the braai (that being beef, lamb, pork and chicken), the useful braai cuts or portions for chicken are by far the easiest to comprehend.

A whole chicken can quite easily be braaied and all of it can be eaten at the braai or on any given day at home. A whole cow, lamb or pig – not so much. As with the other three, the chicken is quite symmetrical, meaning it comes standard with two of each useful cut. There are eight largely accepted, useful cuts of meat on a chicken: two drumsticks, two thighs, two wings and two breasts.

If you debone the breast meat or cut it out of the carcass and pull the skin off, that is commonly referred to as a 'chicken breast fillet'. A chicken breast fillet is from an entirely different part of the animal than its namesake (the beef fillet from a cow). They do have some characteristics in common: both are very lean cuts of meat with relatively little flavour compared to some other cuts from the same animals, for instance. But whereas a beef fillet is famed for being the most tender of the widely braaied cuts of steak, a chicken fillet cannot stake a claim to that characteristic. A chicken breast fillet is, in fact, so lean that it can easily be overcooked and become quite tough.

Compounding this potential problem is the fact that most chicken breasts arrive at your braai with a bit of an attitude. The plump part of that raw chicken breast fillet is somewhat tight, contracted and stiff – and I use all three of these words in their bad sense. You must fix this problem by simply beating their attitude out of them with a meat mallet or any other suitably weighted object, like a bottle of wine.

Place the chicken breast fillets on a chopping board; in this case, preferably a plastic chopping board. I prefer a plastic chopping board for this because then you can pop it into the dishwasher straight afterwards. Wooden chopping boards are obviously nicer to serve food on and look better on your social media photos – but you should never ever serve raw chicken or post photos of it on social media.

So, when tenderising the chicken breasts, we just want them to drop their attitude, not turn them into chicken mince, so place them with the rougher side facing the chopping board (that is the side formerly attached to the chicken carcass). You want the shiny side of each facing upwards (that is the side that the skin used to be attached to). Next, you cover them with cling wrap if you're indoors, so as to prevent microscopic pieces of chicken meat flying all over your kitchen and attracting flies. Outdoors, I find covering with cling wrap is unnecessary. Now give the plump part of each chicken breast fillet a few whacks with your suitably weighted weapon of choice until you can see and feel the piece of meat relax, similar to a muscle relaxing when massaged. Remove and discard the cling wrap.

This exercise makes the piece of meat more uniform in thickness and thus easier to braai evenly. It also creates the odd crack and tear and similar spaces in the meat, making it more receptive to the salts, herbs, spices and sauces you're going to give it. Finally, as the meat is less tough, this practice makes it a much more pleasant thing to eat, especially in a burger.

There are many recipes in this book that specifically call for chicken breast fillets to be braaied as the patties in those recipes, but for all other regulation beef burger recipes in the book, you can also swap the beef patties for chicken breast fillets if that's your preference.

Remember: always take everything in this book with a pinch of braai salt. In that spirit, it delights me to say that during the final stages of publishing this book, we reached a global agreement (with all multinational poultry farming role players, representatives from small-scale farming interests, as well as all major supermarket groups and independent butchery boards) that henceforth, the packaging and sale of chicken breast fillets will be standardised, being sold in packs of four. The burger recipes in this book are designed to serve four, so this four-pack standard for chicken breast fillets is a significant win for all of us.

BRAAIBROODJIES

TRADITIONAL BRAAIBROODJIE

The braaibroodjie is the highlight of many a braai. Those not yet emancipated by the fact that you don't need meat at every braai, frequently braai meat as a pretext when all they actually want is braaibroodjies. This recipe is the traditional way to build a braaibroodjie; you could also refer to it as the 'original'.

This book is filled with many other braaibroodjie recipes, all of them brilliant in their own right. But there is only one *original* recipe for braaibroodjies: they have chutney, onion, tomato, cheese, salt and pepper as filling and they are buttered on the outsides. You do not omit any of these ingredients, nor do you enter into a discussion with an uneducated person who intends to butter them on the insides as opposed to the outsides.

WHAT YOU NEED
(makes 6)

12 bread slices
butter
chutney
240 g Cheddar cheese (sliced or grated)
2 or 3 tomatoes (sliced, 2–3 slices per braaibroodjie)
1 onion (sliced into rings)
salt and pepper

WHAT TO DO

1. Build the braaibroodjies: Spread butter on one side of each slice of bread (these sides will be outward-facing in the assembled braaibroodjie). Place half the bread slices butter-side down; spread chutney on them and evenly distribute all the cheese, tomato and onion on top. Grind salt and pepper over that. Cover with the remaining bread slices, buttered sides facing upwards.
2. '*Braaibroodjies is draaibroodjies*'. Braaibroodjies should be turned often and are braaied in a closed, hinged grid. If you don't have one, buy one – preferably with adjustable heights to compress each unit perfectly. You want medium-paced, gentle heat and the grid should be relatively high. Your aim is for the cheese to be melted and all other fillings to be completely heated by the time the outsides are golden brown. Slightly opening and closing your hinged grid a few times after each of the first few turns of the braai process helps the braaibroodjies not to get stuck to the grid.
3. Once done, slice each braaibroodjie in half. Generally, I believe that the correct way to slice braaibroodjies is diagonally and the correct time to serve is immediately.

AND ...

In recent years, I've sometimes started to spread olive oil onto the outsides of my braaibroodjies as opposed to butter. There is no place in my house for any butter-like substance that is not butter, and real butter is sometimes very hard to spread when straight out of the fridge if you don't time it well, so then I use olive oil. I also prefer it when travelling without a fridge. It's different but also works very well. In most of the recipes in the rest of this book, I specify the option of butter or olive oil on the outsides as both work. For the original though, clearly it's butter. If you make the traditional braaibroodjie with olive oil on the outside as I often do, that is absolutely fine but it's not called original. It's called 'original with olive oil on the outside'.

BILTONG BRAAIBROODJIE

South Africa's favourite fireside snack inside South Africa's favourite braai snack.

WHAT YOU NEED
(makes 6)

12 bread slices
butter or olive oil
2 red onions (sliced)
1 tot soft brown sugar
1 tot balsamic vinegar
1 cup (about 200 g) **biltong** (finely chopped)
plain cream cheese (1 tub will be enough)
240 g Cheddar cheese (sliced or grated)

WHAT TO DO

1. Heat some butter or oil in your pan and fry the onion until soft. Add the sugar and balsamic to the onions and let it simmer over low heat for about 15–20 minutes until the onions are sweet and sticky. Set aside to cool.
2. Use your most aggressive, biggest and sharpest knife to chop the biltong finely. If you don't have a knife that in any way fits into this description, buy one.
3. Build the braaibroodjies: Spread butter or olive oil on one side of each slice of bread (these sides will be outward-facing in the assembled braaibroodjie). Pack half these slices buttered-side down and spread cream cheese on all the slices. Then add a layer of caramelised onions and biltong. Cover with a layer of Cheddar cheese. Close the braaibroodjies with the remaining bread slices, buttered sides facing upwards.
4. '*Braaibroodjies is draaibroodjies*'. Braaibroodjies should be turned often and are braaied in a closed, hinged grid. If you don't have one, buy one – preferably with adjustable heights to compress each unit perfectly. You want medium-paced, gentle heat and the grid should be relatively high. Your aim is for the cheese to be melted and all other fillings to be completely heated by the time the outsides are golden brown. Slightly opening and closing your hinged grid a few times after each of the first few turns of the braai process helps the braaibroodjies not to get stuck to the grid.
5. Once done, slice each braaibroodjie in half. Generally, I believe that the correct way to slice braaibroodjies is diagonally and the correct time to serve is immediately.

AND ...

Here, even a casual attempt will result in quite a good braaibroodjie but attention to detail will make all the difference. Start off with caramelised onions that you're proud of. They should be so good that you want to eat all of them before adding them to the braaibroodjies – but don't. Also chop the biltong quite fine – the finer the better. This makes a big difference to the ease and enjoyment of eating the braaibroodjie. We're not looking for that biltong dust you can buy commercially (that would be too fine); we're looking for actual slices of biltong, chopped finely.

THE SUPERMODEL

For the cover of this book, we needed a supermodel. Now, unlike beauty and fashion magazines in the days when beauty and fashion magazines existed, you cannot simply phone up the managers and agents of superstar braaibroodjie cover model agents. The greatest braaibroodjies in the world are all in this book. The book you are holding is the catalogue of models. And so my colleagues and I (the 'Jan Braai Dream Team' as I call them – without whom this book would not have been possible) set about to create a supermodel braaibroodjie, fit for the cover of this book. This is it.

WHAT YOU NEED
(makes 6)

12 bread slices
butter or olive oil
1 red onion (sliced)
1 green bell pepper (sliced)
1 yellow bell pepper (sliced)
2 wheels (about 150 g) **feta cheese** (crumbled)
240 g Cheddar cheese (sliced or grated)
3 big red tomatoes (sliced)
salt and pepper
1 tot fresh parsley (stemmed and chopped)

WHAT TO DO

1. Build the braaibroodjies: Spread butter or olive oil on one side of each slice of bread (these sides will be outward-facing in the assembled braaibroodjie). Pack half these slices buttered-side down and layer with red onion and peppers, feta cheese, Cheddar cheese and tomato slices. Season with salt, pepper and parsley. Close the braaibroodjies with the remaining bread slices, buttered sides facing upwards.

2. '*Braaibroodjies is draaibroodjies*'. Braaibroodjies should be turned often and are braaied in a closed, hinged grid. If you don't have one, buy one – preferably with adjustable heights to compress each unit perfectly. You want medium-paced, gentle heat and the grid should be relatively high. Your aim is for the cheese to be melted and all other fillings to be completely heated by the time the outsides are golden brown. Slightly opening and closing your hinged grid a few times after each of the first few turns of the braai process helps the braaibroodjies not to get stuck to the grid.

3. Once done, slice each braaibroodjie in half. Generally, I believe that the correct way to slice braaibroodjies is diagonally and the correct time to serve is immediately.

CHORIZO BRAAIBROODJIE

Chorizo is a flavour profile on its own. We're going for a braaibroodjie with its greatest elements (golden-brown, braaied, fire-infused bread and melted cheese) playing a supporting role and simply letting the chorizo shine. You can add everything your know-it-all 'foodie' friend can randomly dream up into this one and end up calling it the Paella Braaibroodjie, but that's really not what we're after. Keep it simple and stick to the ingredients below. And when someone suggests you also add ... stop them there.

WHAT YOU NEED
(makes 6)

12 bread slices
butter or olive oil
1 chorizo sausage
(the cured type)
240 g Cheddar cheese
(sliced or grated)
1 onion (sliced or chopped)

WHAT TO DO

1. Thinly slice the chorizo or chop it up.
2. Build the braaibroodjies: Spread butter or olive oil on one side of each slice of bread (these sides will be outward-facing in the assembled braaibroodjie). Pack half these slices buttered-side down and layer with the cheese, chorizo and onion. Close the braaibroodjies with the remaining bread slices, buttered sides facing upwards.
3. '*Braaibroodjies is draaibroodjies*'. Braaibroodjies should be turned often and are braaied in a closed, hinged grid. If you don't have one, buy one – preferably with adjustable heights to compress each unit perfectly. You want medium-paced, gentle heat and the grid should be relatively high. Your aim is for the cheese to be melted and all other fillings to be completely heated by the time the outsides are golden brown. Slightly opening and closing your hinged grid a few times after each of the first few turns of the braai process helps the braaibroodjies not to get stuck to the grid.
4. Once done, slice each braaibroodjie in half. Generally I believe that the correct way to slice braaibroodjies is diagonally and the correct time to serve is immediately. In this case you serve it with sangria.

AND ...

My recipe for sangria is to chop up 1 apple and 1 orange, and that goes into a jug. Add to that a generous dash of brandy, a cup of orange juice and 2 cups of red wine. Mix all of this together and fill the jug with ice. Now top this up with lemonade or soda water.

BACON AND BANANA BRAAIBROODJIE

If, from the name of this one, it's not strikingly apparent to you exactly how good it tastes, then you are exactly the type of ignoramus who should make an effort to enlighten yourself and find out. Most readers of this book do not fall into this prior category though because reading or flipping through a book filled with burger and braaibroodjie recipes already sets the bar at awesome.

Almost the only thing to mention here is that you should use bananas in their prime. Banana bread is the one you bake with bananas at the end of their useful life. Banana braaibroodjies are a higher level of being and here, you want to use the fruit when it's as close to its prime as possible, or slightly beyond that. Secondly, you need to fry the bananas in butter or oil before they go into the braaibroodjies. Same with the bacon – you braai that first. You don't use raw bacon and neither do you use raw bananas. Braaied and fried. Nothing else to it. This will be one of the easier wins of your life.

WHAT YOU NEED
(makes 6)

12 bread slices
butter or olive oil
1 packet bacon
6 bananas (peeled and butterflied)
golden syrup
240 g Cheddar cheese (sliced or grated)

WHAT TO DO

1. Cook the bacon and banana first, before building your braaibroodjie. Bacon must be cooked crispy. The easiest and tastiest way to achieve this is on a braai grid over the coals. Lay the pieces out carefully, so that they don't fall through the grid, and only turn them once on the braai. Remove from the fire when ready.
2. Fry the butterflied banana pieces in a bit of oil or butter until they are soft. I butterfly, in other words, slice each banana in half lengthwise but if you simply slice them into circular pieces as you would for banana salad with your curry, that would also work – you will just have more pieces to manage when frying them.
3. Build the braaibroodjies: Spread butter or olive oil on one side of each slice of bread (these sides will be outward-facing in the assembled braaibroodjie). Pack half these slices buttered-side down, layer with the bacon and bananas and drizzle the syrup over. Cover with Cheddar cheese. Close the braaibroodjies with the remaining bread slices, buttered sides facing upwards.
4. '*Braaibroodjies is draaibroodjies*'. Braaibroodjies should be turned often and are braaied in a closed, hinged grid. If you don't have one, buy one – preferably with adjustable heights to compress each unit perfectly. You want medium-paced, gentle heat and the grid should be relatively high. Your aim is for the cheese to be melted and all other fillings to be completely heated by the time the outsides are golden brown. Slightly opening and closing your hinged grid a few times after each of the first few turns of the braai process helps the braaibroodjies not to get stuck to the grid.
5. Once done, slice each braaibroodjie in half. Generally, I believe that the correct way to slice braaibroodjies is diagonally and the correct time to serve is immediately.

SPANAKOPITA BRAAIBROODJIE

The word spanakopita can literally be translated as 'spinach pie' and is, of course, a very famous and popular Greek dish. Meatwise, there is quite a strong culinary connotation between lamb meat and Greece as well. In South Africa, the braai combination of lamb chops and braaibroodjies is also quite iconic. No surprises then that the spinach-and-feta-based braaibroodjie is a winner. The ingredients below are pretty regulation for a spanakopita, apart from swapping phyllo or pie pastry in the pie variation for sliced bread in my braaibroodjie take. The steps are pretty similar too – right up to brushing or spreading butter or olive oil on the outside (you would do that with the original as well).

WHAT YOU NEED
(makes 6)

12 bread slices
butter or olive oil
1 onion (chopped)
2 garlic cloves (crushed and chopped)
400 g baby spinach (or normal spinach, finely sliced)
200 g feta cheese (crumbled)
240 g Cheddar cheese (sliced or grated)
salt and pepper

WHAT TO DO

1. Heat a tot of oil or butter in your pan and fry the onion and garlic until soft. Add the spinach and fry for a few minutes until it is wilted and half the size, and any excess water it released has cooked off.
2. Remove from the heat, add the crumbled feta and mix well. Season with salt and pepper.
3. Build the braaibroodjies: Spread butter or olive oil on one side of each slice of bread (these sides will be outward-facing in the assembled braaibroodjie). Pack half these slices buttered-side down and layer with the spinach mixture and Cheddar cheese. Close the braaibroodjies with the remaining bread slices, buttered sides facing upwards.
4. *Braaibroodjies is draaibroodjies*. Braaibroodjies should be turned often and are braaied in a closed, hinged grid. If you don't have one, buy one – preferably with adjustable heights to compress each unit perfectly. You want medium-paced, gentle heat and the grid should be relatively high. Your aim is for the cheese to be melted and all other fillings to be completely heated by the time the outsides are golden brown. Slightly opening and closing your hinged grid a few times after each of the first few turns of the braai process helps the braaibroodjies not to get stuck to the grid.
5. Once done, slice each braaibroodjie in half. Generally, I believe that the correct way to slice braaibroodjies is diagonally and the correct time to serve is immediately.

AND …

A note on the spinach: I use packs of baby spinach because I find it visually appealing at the outset of the process, but after cooking, it obviously all looks the same. Then I specify 400 g because at the time of writing this book, baby spinach is commonly sold in such pack sizes in South Africa. This is not an exact science though and if you read this recipe many years after publication and retailers then pack baby spinach in 350 g or 500 g packs, naturally that will also work. The idea is not to whip out a kitchen scale and measure this precisely. Same goes for my suggested quantities of feta and Cheddar – it's how supermarkets often sell it, at the time of writing, and consequently, how I suggest you use it. One pack and the whole pack – whatever ballpark figure that pack size might be.

BREAKFAST BRAAIBROODJIE

Start your day off well.

WHAT YOU NEED
(makes 6)

12 bread slices
butter or olive oil
1 pack bacon
6 eggs
240 g Cheddar cheese (grated)
chutney
2–3 tomatoes (sliced, 2–3 slices per braaibroodjie)
1 onion (sliced into rings)
salt and pepper

WHAT TO DO

1. The bacon must be cooked crispy. The easiest and tastiest way to achieve this is on a braai grid over the coals. Lay the pieces out carefully, so that they don't fall through the grid, and only turn them once on the braai. You can braai bacon over hotter coals than braaibroodjies so chronologically, this will work out well. Remove from the fire when ready, and chop roughly.
2. In a pan or potjie on the fire, scramble the eggs. Everyone has their own style. I usually add some butter, olive oil and all the eggs to the potjie before going to the fire. I also don't like to over-scramble, as I like a bit of white and yellow detail in my scrambled eggs. As it starts to solidify, mix in half of the grated cheese. When almost ready, immediately proceed to the next step.
3. Build the braaibroodjies: Spread butter or olive oil on one side of each slice of bread (these sides will be outward-facing in the assembled braaibroodjie). Place half the bread slices butter-side down, spread chutney on them and evenly distribute all the tomato and onion on top. Grind salt and pepper over that. The expert-level braaier will do all this whilst braaing the bacon and scrambling the eggs. Now, add the scrambled egg on top of this and then equally distribute the remaining half of the grated cheese. Lastly, add the braaied and roughly chopped bacon. Cover with the remaining bread slices, buttered sides facing upwards.
4. '*Braaibroodjies is draaibroodjies*'. Braaibroodjies should be turned often and are braaied in a closed, hinged grid. If you don't have one, buy one – preferably with adjustable heights to compress each unit perfectly. You want medium-paced, gentle heat and the grid should be relatively high. Your aim is for the cheese to be melted and all other fillings to be completely heated by the time the outsides are golden brown. Starting off with warm scrambled eggs inside the braaibroodjies will boost your chances of success. Slightly opening and closing your hinged grid a few times after each of the first few turns of the braai process helps the braaibroodjies not to get stuck to the grid.
5. Once done, slice each braaibroodjie in half. Generally, I believe that the correct way to slice braaibroodjies is diagonally and the correct time to serve is immediately. In this case with coffee.

CURRY MINCE BRAAIBROODJIE

A jaffle is an ancient part of South Africa's culinary and braai heritage. There are many options for fillings but the original and most popular is the curry mince jaffle. In my opinion, driving around with a jaffle iron in your boot is obviously unnecessary if you own a hinged grid and can just as easily make braaibroodjies. I like to prepare this recipe for a road trip or picnic braai. You make the curry mince at home and pack that in a container, which travels with the rest of the ingredients and your braai equipment. The meal you can then prepare on the road or in a remote location is very tasty and impressive in relation to what you have available in the surroundings.

WHAT YOU NEED
(makes 6)

12 bread slices
butter or olive oil
1 onion (chopped)
500 g lean beef mince
2 garlic cloves (crushed and chopped)
1 tsp salt
1 tsp pepper
1 tot medium curry powder
1 tin or sachet tomato paste (around 50 g)
1 tot apricot jam
240 g white Cheddar cheese (sliced or grated)

WHAT TO DO

1. In a potjie or pan, fry the onion in 1 tot of olive oil for a few minutes. Then add the beef mince and garlic, season with salt and pepper, and fry until the meat is cooked and browned. Use your wooden spoon to break up any lumps of meat. Now add the curry powder, tomato paste and apricot jam, and continue to stir and fry until you're happy with what you see, at which point you can remove the potjie or pan from the heat. If you overcooked it and the mince is dry to the point of burning, add a dash of water, wine or beer.

2. Build the braaibroodjies: Spread butter or olive oil on one side of each slice of bread (these sides will be outward-facing in the assembled braaibroodjie). Pack half these slices buttered-side down and evenly distribute the curry mince and then the grated cheese on these. I suggest white Cheddar because it contrasts better with the curry mince but yellow Cheddar will also work. Close the braaibroodjies with the remaining bread slices, buttered sides facing upwards.

3. '*Braaibroodjies is draaibroodjies*'. Braaibroodjies should be turned often and are braaied in a closed, hinged grid. If you don't have one, buy one – preferably with adjustable heights to compress each unit perfectly. You want medium-paced, gentle heat and the grid should be relatively high. Your aim is for the cheese to be melted and all other fillings to be completely heated by the time the outsides are golden brown. Slightly opening and closing your hinged grid a few times after each of the first few turns of the braai process helps the braaibroodjies not to get stuck to the grid. With these braaibroodjies, you will find some of the filling juices visibly seeping through the bread slices during the braai, creating a wonderful colour on one or both sides of the end product, and when braaied perfectly, adding a very nice, crispy, almost crouton-like level of crust.

4. Once done, slice each braaibroodjie in half. Generally, I believe that the correct way to slice braaibroodjies is diagonally and the correct time to serve is immediately.

GREEK-STYLE BRAAIBROODJIE

Two of the most popular side dishes to the South African braai are the traditional braaibroodjie and a Greek salad. They usually meet on the plate. But then, I decided, rather let some of the ingredients meet a bit earlier. It was a very successful meeting. You take some ingredients of a Greek salad and add them into your braaibroodjie. To make it work, you sauté the onion and green pepper in a bit of olive oil beforehand. This sweetens them and serves the dual purpose of making it easier to fit everything into the braaibroodjies. Olives, feta, tomatoes and Cheddar cheese complete the picture. These braaibroodjies are quite bulky and need to be braaied with care. Best practice is to use a hinged grid of adjustable width.

WHAT YOU NEED
(makes 6)

12 bread slices
butter or olive oil
1 green bell pepper (sliced)
1 red onion (sliced)
½ cup olives (halved and pitted)
2 wheels (about 150 g) **feta cheese** (crumbled)
240 g Cheddar cheese (sliced or grated)
3 big red tomatoes (sliced)
salt and pepper
1 tot fresh oregano (stemmed and chopped)

WHAT TO DO

1. Heat some butter or oil in a pan and sauté the pepper and onion until soft and caramelised. This will take about 15 minutes, so be patient.
2. Build the braaibroodjies: Spread butter or olive oil on one side of each slice of bread (these sides will be outward-facing in the assembled braaibroodjie). Pack half these slices buttered-side down and layer with olives, sautéed onion and green pepper, feta cheese, Cheddar cheese and tomato slices. Season with salt, pepper and oregano. Close the braaibroodjies with the remaining bread slices, buttered sides facing upwards.
3. '*Braaibroodjies is draaibroodjies*'. Braaibroodjies should be turned often and are braaied in a closed, hinged grid. If you don't have one, buy one – preferably with adjustable heights to compress each unit perfectly. You want medium-paced, gentle heat and the grid should be relatively high. Your aim is for the cheese to be melted and all other fillings to be completely heated by the time the outsides are golden brown. Slightly opening and closing your hinged grid a few times after each of the first few turns of the braai process helps the braaibroodjies not to get stuck to the grid.
4. Once done, slice each braaibroodjie in half. Generally, I believe that the correct way to slice braaibroodjies is diagonally and the correct time to serve is immediately.

AND ...

Although an ingredient of Greek salad, cucumbers are not welcome in these braaibroodjies. Rather serve it as garnish on the side. A real Greek salad never contains lettuce so you don't need lettuce in either the braaibroodjies or on the side. Apart from the cucumber then, these braaibroodjies contain all the ingredients of a braaibroodjie and a Greek salad. This means that you can serve it as the only and exclusive side to meat at a braai. It's delicious, completely multipurpose and cuts out those annoying untouched bowls of salad at the braai.

HOLY TRINITY BRAAIBROODJIE

Some things work very well together, with the whole being significantly more than the sum of the parts; for example, gin, tonic, ice and a slice of lemon – or the Springbok team winning the 2019 Rugby World Cup. So it is with onions, carrots and celery. These three combine particularly well to create a base flavour profile for a potjie and many other non-fire-related meals. It just works. And so in recognition and to honour the massive role they play in the culinary industry, here is a braaibroodjie where they are not the unseen and unspoken-of foundation of something else that shines. Those in the know will not be surprised to learn that this dedicated braaibroodjie of onion, carrot and celery hits all the right spots on all the right taste buds.

WHAT YOU NEED
(makes 6)

12 bread slices
butter or olive oil
2 onions (chopped)
2 carrots (grated)
celery (equal in length to the carrots, chopped)
salt and pepper
240 g Cheddar cheese (sliced or grated)

WHAT TO DO

1. Using a fireproof pan or cast-iron pot, heat the oil or butter. Add the chopped onion, carrot and celery, and sauté for about 15 minutes until soft and sweet. Vitally important: as the whole braaibroodjie rests on these ingredients, proper seasoning will make all the difference. We're not looking to flash-fry the onions, carrots and celery. They need to casually develop flavour and they need the right amount of salt and pepper. Check the seasoning and add salt and pepper to taste.
2. Build the braaibroodjies: Spread butter or olive oil on one side of each slice of bread (these sides will be outward-facing in the assembled braaibroodjie). Pack half these slices buttered-side down and layer with the carrot mixture and Cheddar cheese. Close the braaibroodjies with the remaining bread slices, buttered sides facing upwards.
3. *'Braaibroodjies is draaibroodjies'*. Braaibroodjies should be turned often and are braaied in a closed, hinged grid. If you don't have one, buy one – preferably with adjustable heights to compress each unit perfectly. You want medium-paced, gentle heat and the grid should be relatively high. Your aim is for the cheese to be melted and all other fillings to be completely heated by the time the outsides are golden brown.
4. Once done, slice each braaibroodjie in half. Generally I believe that the correct way to slice braaibroodjies is diagonally and the correct time to serve is immediately.

braaibroodjies is draaibroodjies

BREAK-TIME BRAAIBROODJIE

When you're braaing, staring into the orange flames of a fire, you are taking a break from life. Similarly, when you are taking a break in the classical sense of the word, at school or work, you literally are taking a break. And so I conclude that braaing and taking a break are similar spiritual animals. Naturally, then, one of the most iconic break-time sandwiches should be done in braaibroodjie format. The Marmite/Bovril and cheese sandwich does not have to be your ultimate favourite; you just need to have developed the basic palate to appreciate that it's a very good flavour combination, hitting many of the right parts of your tongue at the right time.

Use this concept as a braaibroodjie though – buttered on the outsides and braaied golden brown on the heat of coals from your fire, adding a smoky golden crust and perfectly melted cheese centre – and you are hitting not just many but all of the right taste buds at exactly the right time. Take a break – eat a braaibroodjie!

WHAT YOU NEED
(makes 6)

12 bread slices
butter or olive oil
Marmite or Bovril
240 g Cheddar cheese
(sliced or grated)

WHAT TO DO

1. Build the braaibroodjies: Spread butter or olive oil on one side of each slice of bread (these sides will be outward-facing in the assembled braaibroodjie). Pack half these slices buttered-side down and spread with a normal amount of Marmite or Bovril, and top that with Cheddar cheese. Close the braaibroodjies with the remaining bread slices, buttered-sides facing upwards.
2. '*Braaibroodjies is draaibroodjies*'. Braaibroodjies should be turned often and are braaied in a closed, hinged grid. If you don't have one, buy one – preferably with adjustable heights to compress each unit perfectly. You want medium-paced, gentle heat and the grid should be relatively high. Your aim is for the cheese to be melted by the time the outsides are golden brown. Slightly opening and closing your hinged grid a few times after each of the first few turns of the braai process helps the braaibroodjies not to get stuck to the grid.
3. Once done, slice each braaibroodjie in half. Generally, I believe that the correct way to slice braaibroodjies is diagonally and the correct time to serve is immediately.

THREE-CHEESE BRAAIBROODJIE

The South African braaibroodjie has evolved, taking on a life of its own. The original recipe (page 20) will always be a crowd-pleaser and World Cup winner, but the new democratic South Africa has found that there are many other fantastic ways to make braaibroodjies and now it even has its own braaibroodjie recipe book.

This recipe is a celebration of the basic braaibroodjie's core ingredient – cheese. The wider the variety of cheese, the better. For the ingredients list of this recipe, I have specified three types of cheese that are widely available but if you have other types on hand in your fridge, use those. As a basic guideline, you might want to include something very mild like normal mozzarella or Gouda; something more strong and hard like aged Cheddar or the Parmesan hiding in your fridge; and then something creamy or pungent like Camembert or blue cheese. You're aiming for about 50 g cheese or slightly north of that per braaibroodjie. Experiment and make this recipe your own.

WHAT YOU NEED
(makes 6)

12 bread slices
butter or olive oil
1 tot mustard
1 tot mayonnaise
120 g aged Cheddar cheese (sliced or grated)
120 g mozzarella (sliced or grated)
100 g blue cheese (crumbled)

WHAT TO DO

1. Build the braaibroodjies: Spread butter or olive oil on one side of each slice of bread (these sides will be outward-facing in the assembled braaibroodjie). Pack half these slices buttered-side down and spread with a layer of mustard and mayonnaise. Evenly distribute all the cheese onto the slices of the mustard-coated bread. Close the braaibroodjies with the remaining bread slices, buttered sides facing upwards.

2. '*Braaibroodjies is draaibroodjies*'. Braaibroodjies should be turned often and are braaied in a closed, hinged grid. If you don't have one, buy one – preferably with adjustable heights to compress each unit perfectly. You want medium-paced, gentle heat and the grid should be relatively high. Your aim is for the cheese to be melted by the time the outsides are golden brown. Slightly opening and closing your hinged grid a few times after each of the first few turns of the braai process helps the braaibroodjies not to get stuck to the grid.

3. Once done, slice each braaibroodjie in half. Generally, I believe that the correct way to slice braaibroodjies is diagonally and the correct time to serve is immediately.

WEST COAST BRAAIBROODJIE

Bokkoms are a true South African delicacy – think of it as fish biltong. The smell of this salted mullet fish, which is dried in the sun and the salty sea air with a hint of fermented kelp carried on a brisk south-easter wind, is the signature scent of holiday on the idyllic West Coast of South Africa. Bokkoms are such a classic part of South Africa's West Coast heritage that it's tough to imagine the one without the other. The meat has a much more subtle taste than its overpowering smell might indicate and works very well in combination with the ingredients of this recipe. Bokkoms are often sold in bunches.

* You need half a cup of finely chopped bokkom flesh for this recipe. For that you will need about three bokkoms which must then be peeled and deboned by a local West Coast expert. Alternatively, buy some peeled bokkoms (some supermarkets sell them) and cut off the usable flesh part yourself. Lastly, many supermarkets, fish shops and farm stalls in the bokkom-producing region of South Africa sell packs of bokkom fillets, which is definitely your road of least resistance as you then just need to chop them up finely.

WHAT YOU NEED
(makes 6)

12 bread slices
butter or olive oil
2 onions (sliced)
2 tots balsamic vinegar
1 tub sun-dried tomatoes (200–300 g drained and chopped)
½ cup bokkom flesh (from about 3 peeled and deboned bokkoms, finely chopped)*
½ cup olives (pitted and chopped)
½ cup pine nuts (about 50 g)
240 g mozzarella cheese (sliced or grated)
ground black pepper

WHAT TO DO

1. Heat oil or butter in a pan and fry the onions for a few minutes until they get some colour. Add the balsamic vinegar and simmer for another few minutes until the onions are caramelised, soft and sticky. Remove the pan from the heat.
2. Build the braaibroodjies: Spread butter or olive oil on one side of each slice of bread (these sides will be outward-facing in the assembled braaibroodjie). Pack half these slices buttered-side down. Add a layer of sticky caramelised onions to the six slices, then the chopped sun-dried tomatoes, chopped bits of bokkom, olives, pine nuts and cheese. Grind black pepper over this and then close the braaibroodjies with the remaining bread slices, buttered or oiled sides facing upwards.
3. '*Braaibroodjies is draaibroodjies*'. Braaibroodjies should be turned often and are braaied in a closed, hinged grid. If you don't have one, buy one – preferably with adjustable heights to compress each unit perfectly. You want medium-paced, gentle heat and the grid should be relatively high. Your aim is for the cheese to be melted and all other fillings to be completely heated by the time the outsides are golden brown. Slightly opening and closing your hinged grid a few times after each of the first few turns of the braai process helps the braaibroodjies not to get stuck to the grid.
4. Once done, slice each braaibroodjie in half. Generally, I believe that the correct way to slice braaibroodjies is diagonally and the correct time to serve is immediately.

CLUB BRAAIBROODJIE

A braaibroodjie is your chance in life to have the bread buttered on both sides. The Club Braaibroodjie is more than that: it's a double-braaied triple braaibroodjie. There are two braais involved because we first braai the chicken and the bacon for the filling. So you have the taste of braai inside of the braaibroodjie. Then we braai the built braaibroodjies and subsequently triple-stack them with layers of avo and tomato in between. Counting the chicken, bacon and all the outer crusts of braaibroodjies, this gives us 12 layers of braai flavour per portion.

WHAT YOU NEED
(makes 6)

18 bread slices
butter or olive oil
4 chicken breast fillets
braai or chicken spice
1 packet bacon
½ cup mayonnaise
1 medium-sized onion (chopped)
3 gherkins (chopped)
1 tot chutney
1 tot mustard (mild)
1 tsp salt
1 tsp black pepper
240 g cheese (Cheddar, Gouda or similar, grated)
4 tomatoes (sliced)
2 avocados (peeled and mashed)
6 skewers

WHAT TO DO

1. Spice the chicken breast fillets with your favourite braai or chicken spice or simply with salt and pepper. Now braai the chicken breasts on hot coals, turning often until done. This will take around 8 minutes. During the same time that you braai the chicken breasts, also braai the bacon on the grid over the same hot coals. You only need to turn each piece of bacon once. Bacon braais very well and becomes beautifully crispy on a braai grid.
2. Now butter 18 slices of bread on one side and lay half of those slices, buttered-side down, on a tray.
3. Slice, chop or otherwise shred the four braaied chicken breasts and mix that with the mayonnaise, chopped onion and gherkin, chutney, mustard, salt and pepper. Then divide the chicken mayonnaise mix between the nine laid-out slices of bread, spreading it out on each.
4. Evenly distribute the braaied bacon and the grated cheese between the nine slices of chicken-mayonnaise-covered bread. Having chicken mayo mix right on one side and cheese right on the other side will lead to more structure, so order is to some extent important. Cover with the other nine slices of bread, buttered sides facing upwards, to the outside.
5. Put the nine prepared braaibroodjies in a closed, hinged grid and braai over medium coals, turning often until the outsides are golden brown, the insides are heated through and the cheese has melted. Remove from the fire and grid.
6. Distribute half of the avo mash on top of three of the braaied sandwiches and also slices of tomato on each. Top each with another braaied sandwich, then the rest of the avo and tomato. Lastly, add a third braaied sandwich.
7. You should now have three identical towers. Each tower should contain six slices of bread with beautiful layers of chicken mayonnaise, bacon, cheese, avo and tomato somewhere in there. Put two skewers through each tower from the top (one though each half) and now use a big knife to slice each skewered tower in half.
8. Plate the meal with a skewered portion of Club Braaibroodjie per person.

PERI-PERI CHICKEN LIVER BRAAIBROODJIE

Originally, I thought the best place to eat peri-peri chicken livers was in a tavern, with some crusty bread. Then I figured out how to nail the meal on my fire at home and that became my venue of choice for this connoisseur meal. I still served it with crusty bread though. Perfection level has now been reached. First, you prepare the very tasty peri-peri chicken livers on the fire and then use that as the main ingredient for the filling of the braaibroodjies. So we're not serving them with crusty bread any more; we're serving them right in the middle of golden-brown, crispy braaied bread. This one I believe is a meal, more than a side.

WHAT YOU NEED
(makes 6)

FOR THE BRAAIBROODJIE
12 bread slices
butter or olive oil
2 tomatoes (sliced)
240 g Cheddar cheese (sliced or grated)

FOR THE CHICKEN LIVERS
500 g chicken livers
1 tot oil
1 tot butter
1 onion (chopped or sliced)
2 garlic cloves (crushed or finely chopped)
1 red chilli (finely chopped)
1 tot brandy
1 tot paprika
1 tot lemon juice
1 tsp chilli or peri-peri powder

WHAT TO DO

1. Using a fireproof pan or cast-iron pot, start preparing the chicken livers by heating the oil and butter.
2. Add the onion and fry until soft. Add the garlic and chilli and fry for 1 more minute.
3. Add the chicken livers, then fry over high heat for a few minutes until they start to brown on all sides.
4. Next, add the brandy and cook for another minute or two. The brandy may flambé (catch fire), and that's perfectly fine.
5. Add the paprika, lemon juice and chilli powder and then cook for a few minutes, stirring occasionally until the sauce starts to reduce and becomes slightly sticky. During this time, use a knife or fork or sharper-edged spoon or whatever other tool you deem appropriate to convert some of the bigger pieces into smaller pieces, so that you'll have a level and even distribution of chicken liver on the braaibroodjies.
6. When you feel the time is right, take off the fire and let it cool down for a bit.
7. Build the braaibroodjies: Spread butter or olive oil on one side of each slice of bread (these sides will be outward-facing in the assembled braaibroodjie). Pack half these slices buttered-side down and layer with tomatoes, Cheddar cheese and then chicken livers. Close the braaibroodjies with the remaining bread slices, buttered sides facing upwards.
8. '*Braaibroodjies is draaibroodjies*'. Braaibroodjies should be turned often and are braaied in a closed, hinged grid. If you don't have one, buy one – preferably with adjustable heights to compress each unit perfectly. You want medium-paced, gentle heat and the grid should be relatively high. Your aim is for the cheese to be melted and all other fillings to be completely heated by the time the outsides are golden brown. Slightly opening and closing your hinged grid a few times after each of the first few turns of the braai process helps the braaibroodjies not to get stuck to the grid. With these braaibroodjies you will find some of the filling juices visibly seeping through the bread slices during the braai, creating a wonderful colour on one or both sides of the end product – and when braaied perfectly, adding a very nice, crispy, almost crouton-like level of crust.
9. Once done, slice each braaibroodjie in half. Generally, I believe that the correct way to slice braaibroodjies is diagonally and the correct time to serve is immediately.

CHEESE AND HERB BRAAIBROODJIE

This one originates from a braai at the beautiful Gates Waterfall in Transkei. On our way there, we picked a few wild herbs in a forest and built these numbers. No, not the funky herbs that some people smoke – just edible herbs giving flavour to food, growing in the wild. In this case, I believe it's preferable to use white Cheddar so that the herbs present nicely when you're slicing the braaibroodjies and, as always, I suggest using full-cream (also called full-fat) cream cheese as that is the point of cream cheese, is it not?

At the time of writing this book, my favourite and go-to combination of herbs – not only for these braaibroodjies but general use – is oregano and thyme, so that is what I use here and what I think works for the style of this braaibroodjie. But if your garden or fridge supplies you more abundantly with some other herbs, then use those and the end result will just have a different herb flavour.

WHAT YOU NEED
(makes 6)

12 bread slices
butter or olive oil
1 tub (250 g) **cream cheese** (plain, herb flavoured or garlic flavoured)
fresh oregano (stemmed and chopped)
fresh thyme (stemmed and chopped)
1 red onion (sliced)
240 g white Cheddar cheese (sliced or grated)

WHAT TO DO

1. Build the braaibroodjies: Spread butter or olive oil on one side of each slice of bread (these sides will be outward-facing in the assembled braaibroodjie). Pack half these slices buttered-side down and spread with a layer of cream cheese, and add the chopped herbs and sliced onions on top of the cream cheese. Cover with Cheddar cheese. Close the braaibroodjies with the remaining bread slices, buttered sides facing upwards.

2. '*Braaibroodjies is draaibroodjies*'. Braaibroodjies should be turned often and are braaied in a closed, hinged grid. If you don't have one, buy one – preferably with adjustable heights to compress each unit perfectly. You want medium-paced, gentle heat and the grid should be relatively high. Your aim is for the cheese to be melted by the time the outsides are golden brown. Slightly opening and closing your hinged grid a few times after each of the first few turns of the braai process helps the braaibroodjies not to get stuck to the grid.

3. Once done, slice each braaibroodjie in half. Generally, I believe that the correct way to slice braaibroodjies is diagonally and the correct time to serve is immediately.

CHICKEN MAYO BRAAIBROODJIE

Two of my favourite meals (and I'd say this goes for most South Africans) are toasted chicken mayo sandwiches and a traditional braaibroodjie – the one when on the road, and the other around a braai fire. Here, we combine the two and create something truly awesome: a braaibroodjie with a chicken mayo filling. When it comes to mayonnaise, I prefer creamy, also often referred to as 'French style'. It generally comes with a blue colour scheme on the label, as opposed to 'tangy style' whose labels tend to be green. Life's all about choices so decide for yourself.

This recipe originated when I had some leftover braaied chicken, on an occasion when there'd been many guests and everyone had opted for the boerewors and chops. Later on the same day, with most of those guests still present, I decided to employ the braaied chicken in this manner. In real life, you might end up buying rotisserie chicken now and again to prepare this feast from scratch but if ever life serves you leftover braaied chicken, this is your go-to.

WHAT YOU NEED
(makes 6)

12 bread slices
butter or olive oil
1 cooked chicken (braaied or rotisserie)
½ cup mayonnaise
1 medium-sized onion (chopped)
3 gherkins (chopped)
1 tot chutney
1 tot mustard (mild)
1 tot parsley (chopped)
1 tsp salt
1 tsp black pepper

WHAT TO DO

1. Using a pair of capable and clean hands, take all the chicken meat off the bones. It's messy but it's not difficult. Discard the chicken bones and skin.
2. Chop or tear the deboned chicken into smaller chunks.
3. In a large mixing bowl, add all the ingredients, except the bread and butter or oil, to the chunks of chicken and mix well.
4. Build the braaibroodjies: Spread butter or olive oil on one side of each slice of bread (these sides will be outward-facing in the assembled braaibroodjie). Pack half these slices buttered-side down and top with a layer of the chicken mayo filling. Close the braaibroodjies with the remaining bread slices, buttered sides facing upwards.
5. *'Braaibroodjies is draaibroodjies'*. Braaibroodjies should be turned often and are braaied in a closed, hinged grid. If you don't have one, buy one – preferably with adjustable heights to compress each unit perfectly. You want medium-paced, gentle heat and the grid should be relatively high. Your aim is for the filling to be completely heated through by the time the outsides are golden brown. Slightly opening and closing your hinged grid a few times after each of the first few turns of the braai process helps the braaibroodjies not to get stuck to the grid.
6. Once done, slice each braaibroodjie in half. Generally, I believe that the correct way to slice braaibroodjies is diagonally and the correct time to serve is immediately.

AND ...

If you are thinking that this recipe could be improved by adding cheese and bacon, think so quietly and don't tell anybody else you had those thoughts. A properly made Chicken Mayo Braaibroodjie is perfect as is, in the way that a properly made chocolate milkshake is perfect. It does not need to be a triple-chocolate, double-cookie-crusted, deep-fried-doughnut-dipped, cacao-smoked-cream-topped, caramel-glazed, strobe-light jar. For the distinguished braaier with a slightly more pronounced appetite, there is of course the Club Braaibroodjie (page 46).

MUSHROOM BRAAIBROODJIE

Mushrooms impart the savoury fifth-flavour element called umami to any food you add it to. This is a fact. My opinion is that speaking about umami in a recipe, particularly in the introduction of a recipe, is very poncy, so we're not starting off well here. There is method to the madness though, as my point is that this is the reason mushrooms are one of the big-three additions to recipes. It simply does not matter how well balanced, tried, tested and researched a recipe is; there will always be a clown suggesting that it could be improved by adding one of the big three – the big three being bacon, cream and mushrooms. Whatever you do, somebody will want to add one of them.

And so it follows that I don't think we should be adding mushrooms into other well-constructed braaibroodjies. I am of the firm belief that you should simply make a mushroom-dedicated braaibroodjie to let this culinary superstar shine on its own stage. The flavour of mushrooms intensifies when you pan-fry them, so before using them as filling for you braaibroodjie, that is definitely what you want to do.

WHAT YOU NEED
(makes 6)

12 bread slices
butter or olive oil
1 red onion (sliced)
2 punnets (500 g) **mushrooms** (I recommend a mix of portabellini and white button mushrooms, roughly chopped)
2 garlic cloves (crushed and chopped)
ground black pepper
plain cream cheese (1 tub will be enough)
240 g Cheddar cheese (sliced or grated)

WHAT TO DO

1. Heat some butter or oil in a pan on the fire and fry the onion and mushrooms until they go soft and then golden brown. Add the garlic and pepper and fry for another minute.
2. Build the braaibroodjies: Spread butter or olive oil on one side of each slice of bread (these sides will be outward-facing in the assembled braaibroodjie). Pack half these slices buttered-side down and spread cream cheese on all the slices. Then add a layer of the mushroom mixture and Cheddar cheese. Close the braaibroodjies with the remaining bread slices, buttered sides facing upwards.
3. '*Braaibroodjies is draaibroodjies*'. Braaibroodjies should be turned often and are braaied in a closed, hinged grid. If you don't have one, buy one – preferably with adjustable heights to compress each unit perfectly. You want medium-paced, gentle heat and the grid should be relatively high. Your aim is for the cheese to be melted and all other fillings to be completely heated by the time the outsides are golden brown. Slightly opening and closing your hinged grid a few times after each of the first few turns of the braai process helps the braaibroodjies not to get stuck to the grid.
4. Once done, slice each braaibroodjie in half. Generally, I believe that the correct way to slice braaibroodjies is diagonally and the correct time to serve is immediately.

EMPANADA BRAAIBROODJIE

In Argentina, one snack rules them all when standing, or sitting, around the fire waiting for the meat to be ready – the empanada, a distant cousin of the samoosa or cocktail-sized pie. With the most popular cut of meat, the beef short rib, taking half a day to get ready, you can understand why there need to be a few snacks to keep the braaier and assistants going. Now, the empanada can have various fillings, traditionally based on region, with my favourite being the corn and cheese. At the time of writing this book, Argentina is the fourth largest corn producer in the world and I think this is thus a fitting filling for a braaibroodjie paying homage to their asado culture.

The empanada braaibroodjie can stand as a meal in its own right but how I really think you play this one is: braai the mielies golden brown on some side coals whilst you're doing some multi-hour meal like a potjie or lamb spit. Build the braaibroodjies, braai them perfectly and serve as snacks around the fire.

WHAT YOU NEED
(makes 6)

12 bread slices
butter or olive oil
2 mielies
1 tsp cumin
1 tsp paprika
salt and pepper
1 punnet fresh coriander (finely chopped)
1 red onion (sliced)
240 g Cheddar cheese (sliced or grated)

WHAT TO DO

1. Braai the mielies on a braai grid over hot coals, and toast on all sides. Braaied mielies have significantly more flavour than non-braaied mielies. Once charred a bit, remove from the fire and use a sharp knife to cut the kernels off the cob and place into a mixing bowl.
2. Season the charred mielie kernels with cumin, paprika, salt and pepper and mix well so that all the corn is seasoned. Chop the coriander finely and mix into the seasoned mielies.
3. Build the braaibroodjies: Spread butter or olive oil on one side of each slice of bread (these sides will be outward-facing in the assembled braaibroodjie). Pack half these slices buttered-side down and layer with the corn mixture and then red onion slices. Cover with Cheddar cheese. Close the braaibroodjies with the remaining bread slices, buttered sides facing upwards.
4. '*Braaibroodjies is draaibroodjies*'. Braaibroodjies should be turned often and are braaied in a closed, hinged grid. If you don't have one, buy one – preferably with adjustable heights to compress each unit perfectly. You want medium-paced, gentle heat and the grid should be relatively high. Your aim is for the cheese to be melted and all other fillings to be completely heated by the time the outsides are golden brown. Slightly opening and closing your hinged grid a few times after each of the first few turns of the braai process helps the braaibroodjies not to get stuck to the grid.
5. Once done, slice each braaibroodjie in half. Generally, I believe that the correct way to slice braaibroodjies is diagonally and the correct time to serve is immediately.

DELUXE BRAAIBROODJIE

Going big – the braaibroodjie for early in the month, late in the year, when man is at his most flush. A celebration of the braaibroodjie's two core ingredients – cheese and bread.

WHAT YOU NEED
(makes 6)

18 bread slices (3 slices per braaibroodjie)
butter or olive oil
1 pack bacon
1 tot Dijon mustard
1 tot wholegrain mustard
2 tots mayonnaise
1 packet cooked ham (6–12 slices)
400 g cheese (a combination of different cheese also works)

WHAT TO DO

1. The bacon must be cooked crispy. The easiest and tastiest way to achieve this is on a braai grid over the coals. Lay the pieces out carefully, so that they don't fall through the grid, and only turn them once on the braai. You can braai bacon over hotter coals than braaibroodjies so chronologically, this will work out well. Remove from the fire when ready and chop roughly.
2. Build the braaibroodjies: Spread butter or olive oil on one side of each slice of bread and pack 12 of these slices buttered-side down. Mix the mustard and mayonnaise, then spread this mustard-and-mayonnaise mixture onto the 12 slices of bread. Allocate equal amounts of the braaied and roughly chopped bacon to half of the slices (so on six of the mustard-mayonnaise slices). Also, roughly chop the ham and distribute that onto the other six slices. Evenly distribute the cheese onto all 12 slices – onto the bacon-topped slices, as well as ham-topped slices. Place each bacon-containing slice on top of a ham-containing slice and close with the last six remaining slices of bread, buttered sides facing upwards.
3. You should now have double-layered braaibroodjies that go something like: bread, mustard and mayonnaise, ham, cheese, bread, mustard and mayonnaise, bacon, cheese, bread.
4. '*Braaibroodjies is draaibroodjies*'. Braaibroodjies should be turned often and are braaied in a closed, hinged grid. If you don't have one, buy one – preferably with adjustable heights to compress each unit perfectly. You want medium-paced, gentle heat and the grid should be relatively high. Your aim is for the cheese to be melted and all other fillings to be completely heated by the time the outsides are golden brown. Being triple layered, this will be one of your more challenging braaibroodjies, but by making sure your coals are not too hot and by paying attention, it's entirely manageable. Slightly opening and closing your hinged grid a few times after each of the first few turns of the braai process helps the braaibroodjies not to get stuck to the grid.
5. Once done, slice each braaibroodjie in half. Generally, I believe that the correct way to slice braaibroodjies is diagonally and the correct time to serve is immediately.

AND …

This recipe was originally designed to be served with a glass of cold white wine from South Africa's coastal region, but that is really up to you.

FIG AND FETA BRAAIBROODJIE

In the Western Cape, we like to serve things with preserved green figs, and usually there will be cheese involved as well. The odds of being served preserved figs and cheese as a snack before your meal is about as high as being served preserved figs and cheese as dessert (similar, but in a different way, to brandy and coke at many braais in South Africa). It's a flavour combination that simply works. So here we are making the preserved figs and cheese the main actors, right in the centre of the braaibroodjie. No surprises then that the result works equally well as a starter, main meal or dessert!

WHAT YOU NEED
(makes 6)

12 bread slices
butter or olive oil
2 red onions (sliced into rings)
240 g mozzarella cheese (grated)
1 small tub (200 g) **black pepper-flavoured feta cheese** (crumbled)
8 preserved green figs (chopped)

WHAT TO DO

1. Caramelise or brown the sliced onions with a bit of oil or butter in a pan or pot on the fire or stove.
2. Build the braaibroodjies: Spread butter or olive oil on one side of each slice of bread (these sides will be outward-facing in the assembled braaibroodjie). Pack half these slices buttered-side down and evenly distribute the caramelised onions, grated mozzarella, crumbled feta and chopped figs between the six laid-out slices of bread. Close the braaibroodjies with the remaining bread slices, buttered sides facing upwards.
3. *'Braaibroodjies is draaibroodjies'*. Braaibroodjies should be turned often and are braaied in a closed, hinged grid. If you don't have one, buy one – preferably with adjustable heights to compress each unit perfectly. You want medium-paced, gentle heat and the grid should be relatively high. Your aim is for the cheese to be melted and all other fillings to be completely heated by the time the outsides are golden brown. Slightly opening and closing your hinged grid a few times after each of the first few turns of the braai process helps the braaibroodjies not to get stuck to the grid.
4. Once done, slice each braaibroodjie in half. Generally, I believe that the correct way to slice braaibroodjies is diagonally and the correct time to serve is immediately.

CALAMARI BRAAIBROODJIE

On surf and related trips, Calamari Burgers are nothing new: freshly fried calamari on a hamburger roll with some sauce. This recipe is just a more advanced and refined version based on the same principle. We're adding another layer of crisp (the outsides of the braaibroodjies) and a very welcome layer of melted cheese. What you need to pull this one off effortlessly is a portion of warm, freshly fried, tender calamari in close proximity to a place where you can braai. Fortunately, South Africa's vast coastline is completely littered with exactly that – fish and chips shops and public picnic braai areas.

WHAT YOU NEED
(makes 6)

12 bread slices
butter or olive oil
½ cup mayonnaise
2 tomatoes (sliced)
1 onion (sliced)
salt and pepper
1 generous portion of fried calamari (from the fish and chips takeaway shop)
240 g Cheddar cheese (sliced or grated)

WHAT TO DO

1. Build the braaibroodjies: Spread butter or olive oil on one side of each slice of bread (these sides will be outward-facing in the assembled braaibroodjie). Pack half these slices buttered-side down and spread with a layer of mayonnaise, tomato and onion, and season with salt and pepper. Equally distribute the calamari between all of these and cover with cheese. Close the braaibroodjies with the remaining bread slices, buttered sides facing upwards.

2. '*Braaibroodjies is draaibroodjies*'. Braaibroodjies should be turned often and are braaied in a closed, hinged grid. If you don't have one, buy one – preferably with adjustable heights to compress each unit perfectly. You want medium-paced, gentle heat and the grid should be relatively high. Your aim is for the cheese to be melted and all other fillings to be completely heated by the time the outsides are golden brown. Slightly opening and closing your hinged grid a few times after each of the first few turns of the braai process helps the braaibroodjies not to get stuck to the grid.

3. Once done, slice each braaibroodjie in half. Generally, I believe that the correct way to slice braaibroodjies is diagonally and the correct time to serve is immediately.

ANCHOVY, CAPER AND OLIVE BRAAIBROODJIE

The title of this one pretty accurately describes it. This is one of my personal favourites but due to the acquired-taste nature of more than one ingredient, you're either going to love this or should not attempt it at all. I was fortunate enough to grow up in a house with two olive trees in the garden and where puttanesca pasta was a regular dish, so my palate very much appreciates this flavour profile and I am happy to share it with you.

WHAT YOU NEED
(makes 6)

12 bread slices
butter or olive oil
plain cream cheese (1 tub will be enough)
1 small jar anchovy fillets
2 tots capers (drained)
½ cup black olives (pitted and roughly chopped)
1 red onion (sliced)
freshly ground black pepper
240 g Cheddar cheese (sliced or grated)
100 g pine nuts (or roughly chopped cashew nuts, roasted)

WHAT TO DO

1. Build the braaibroodjies: Spread butter or olive oil on one side of each slice of bread (these sides will be outward-facing in the assembled braaibroodjie). Pack half these slices buttered-side down and spread with a layer of cream cheese and equally distribute the anchovies, capers, olives and onions. Season with black pepper. Cover with Cheddar cheese and sprinkle the roasted nuts over the cheese. Close the braaibroodjies with the remaining bread slices, buttered sides facing upwards.
2. '*Braaibroodjies is draaibroodjies*'. Braaibroodjies should be turned often and are braaied in a closed, hinged grid. If you don't have one, buy one – preferably with adjustable heights to compress each unit perfectly. You want medium-paced, gentle heat and the grid should be relatively high. Your aim is for the cheese to be melted and all other fillings to be completely heated by the time the outsides are golden brown. Slightly opening and closing your hinged grid a few times after each of the first few turns of the braai process helps the braaibroodjies not to get stuck to the grid.
3. Once done, slice each braaibroodjie in half. Generally, I believe that the correct way to slice braaibroodjies is diagonally and the correct time to serve is immediately.

SNOEK BRAAIBROODJIE

There is wonderful simplicity to eating braaied snoek. When fresh, braaied properly and paired with a glass of cold white wine, it's a luxury lunch all by itself. Life needs very little after that, apart from an afternoon nap. The snoek braaibroodjie continues this proud tradition of understated luxury and the only challenging part is that you need leftover braaied snoek, which, if you had a fresh, well-braaied snoek, is actually not that easy to achieve as there might not be leftovers. Plan ahead, and failing that, buy smoked snoek from your local fishmonger or supermarket.

WHAT YOU NEED
(makes 6)

12 bread slices
butter or olive oil
about 500 g braaied snoek (or smoked snoek or any other braaied fish that was left over)
½ cup mayonnaise
1 medium-sized onion (chopped)
3 gherkins (chopped)
1 tot chutney
1 tot mustard (mild)
1 tot parsley (chopped)
1 tsp salt (optional)
1 tsp black pepper
2 lemons

WHAT TO DO

1. Remove the fish from the bones and remove any extra bones and skin. This is an important step and it's worth giving it your full and undivided attention. Ensure that no fish bones end up in your filling and consequently get stuck in your or anyone else's throat.
2. In a large mixing bowl, add all the filling ingredients, except the salt, to the chunks of snoek and mix well. That means add the mayonnaise, onion, gherkins, chutney, mustard, parsley and pepper. Taste the mixture and if it needs salt, add that. Whether or not to add salt will largely depend on how much salt the snoek already had and thus contributed to the mixture.
3. Build the braaibroodjies: Spread butter or olive oil on one side of each slice of bread (these sides will be outward-facing in the assembled braaibroodjie). Pack half these slices buttered-side down and spread an equal portion of the snoek mixture on each. Close the braaibroodjies with the remaining bread slices, buttered sides facing upwards.
4. '*Braaibroodjies is draaibroodjies*'. Braaibroodjies should be turned often and are braaied in a closed, hinged grid. If you don't have one, buy one – preferably with adjustable heights to compress each unit perfectly. You want medium-paced, gentle heat and the grid should be relatively high. Your aim is for all the fillings to be completely heated by the time the outsides are golden brown. Slightly opening and closing your hinged grid a few times after each of the first few turns of the braai process helps the braaibroodjies not to get stuck to the grid.
5. Once done, slice each braaibroodjie in half. Generally, I believe that the correct way to slice braaibroodjies is diagonally and the correct time to serve is immediately. The snoek braaibroodjie is served with a wedge of lemon for each discerning guest to squeeze onto their work of art themselves.

BRAAIED BUTTERNUT BRAAIBROODJIE

There is a shortcut in this recipe in that you can conceivably cook peeled and chopped butternut pieces in a pot, build the broodjies, braai them and serve in well under an hour, which would make this a perfect and balanced weeknight family dinner. And I will not frown upon that. But for me, this is more of a lengthy one, and is served as a snack midway through an extensive braai. 'Extensive braai' means you are busy braaing some multi-hour meal like a leg of lamb, beef rib, pork shoulder – or one of those in a potjie. In this multi-hour braai scenario, you would place a butternut and two onions on the coals of your fire. Cook them completely on the coals in their natural state, turning as you go. The outsides will be burnt – discard that – but the rest of it will be wonderfully sweet, caramelised and smoky. Now chop that up and build some braaibroodjies with the addition of the anchor ingredients: bread, butter, cheese, salt and pepper. These, gently braaied till the outsides are golden brown and the cheese has melted, are an outstanding way to keep the hunger at bay till the marathon-braai main course is served.

WHAT YOU NEED
(makes 6)

12 bread slices
butter or olive oil
1 medium-sized butternut
2 onions (with skins on)
salt and pepper
240 g Cheddar cheese (grated)

WHAT TO DO

1. Do not peel your butternut or onions. Place the butternut and onions directly into the coals and let them toast for about 15 minutes each side. After about 30 minutes, when your butternut and onions are black on the outside and soft on the inside, you are ready to move to the next step.
2. Use your tongs and a very sharp knife to cut open the butternut. Remove the pips, but scrape out all the good orange, smoked and cooked flesh into a bowl.
3. Remove the first 2–3 black layers of the onion until you get to the sweet, soft onion inside. Use a sharp knife to chop the onions.
4. Build the braaibroodjies: Spread butter or olive oil on one side of each slice of bread (these sides will be outward-facing in the assembled braaibroodjie). Pack half these slices buttered-side down and layer with a spoonful of butternut on the bread, then season with salt and pepper. Place chopped onions on top and cover with a generous amount of grated cheese. Close the braaibroodjies with the remaining bread slices, buttered sides facing upwards.
5. '*Braaibroodjies is draaibroodjies*'. Braaibroodjies should be turned often and are braaied in a closed, hinged grid. If you don't have one, buy one – preferably with adjustable heights to compress each unit perfectly. You want medium-paced, gentle heat and the grid should be relatively high. Your aim is for the cheese to be melted and all other fillings to be completely heated by the time the outsides are golden brown. Slightly opening and closing your hinged grid a few times after each of the first few turns of the braai process helps the braaibroodjies not to get stuck to the grid.
6. Once done, slice each braaibroodjie in half. Generally, I believe that the correct way to slice braaibroodjies is diagonally and the correct time to serve is immediately.

RACLETTE BRAAIBROODJIE

Simply, preparing raclette is nothing but taking a block of cheese, melting it with the heat of the fire, scraping the melted cheese off the block and eating it. So we're dealing with fire-melted cheese – not far off the braaibroodjie mark. After establishing this baseline, coming up with this recipe was a simple matter of heading into wooden mountain huts in the Swiss Alps and sampling all the other supporting actors found at a present-day raclette feast to see which would be beneficial to the Raclette Braaibroodjie.

WHAT YOU NEED
(makes 6)

12 bread slices
butter or olive oil
gherkins (sliced or chopped)
pickled onions (sliced or chopped)
240 g raclette cheese (sliced or grated – Gruyère cheese also fits well and failing that, use the good old braaibroodjie faithful: aged white Cheddar)
6 slices cooked ham
salt and pepper
1 tot Dijon mustard

WHAT TO DO

1. The Raclette Braaibroodjie has two minor challenges; the first, a logistical one: locating raclette cheese and the second, an intellectual one: deciding how many gherkins and how many pickled onions to use. Gherkins and pickled onions vary so widely in size that I do not even specify how many you need in the ingredients part of this recipe, but I am confident that whatever container, most likely a glass jar, you bought these in, there will be more than enough. Don't use all of them!
2. Once you've decided how many gherkins and pickled onions will be enough for your braaibroodjies, slice or chop them. Also slice or grate the cheese.
3. Build the braaibroodjies: Spread butter or olive oil on one side of each slice of bread (these sides will be outward-facing in the assembled braaibroodjie). Pack half these slices buttered-side down and layer with the cheese, ham, gherkins and onions. Add salt and pepper if you're autocondimental. Spread mustard on the non-buttered 'insides' of the remaining bread slices and close the braaibroodjies with buttered sides facing upwards.
4. '*Braaibroodjies is draaibroodjies*'. Braaibroodjies should be turned often and are braaied in a closed, hinged grid. If you don't have one, buy one – preferably with adjustable heights to compress each unit perfectly. You want medium-paced, gentle heat and the grid should be relatively high. Your aim is for the cheese to be melted and all other fillings to be completely heated by the time the outsides are golden brown. Slightly opening and closing your hinged grid a few times after each of the first few turns of the braai process helps the braaibroodjies not to get stuck to the grid.
5. Once done, slice each braaibroodjie in half. Generally, I believe that the correct way to slice braaibroodjies is diagonally and the correct time to serve is immediately.

MACARONI AND CHEESE BRAAIBROODJIE

There will inevitably be some non-believer who's sceptical about this one, and honestly, I am not even going to bother with you. Just make yourself a cup of green tea and move along to the next page. As all intelligent readers attuned to the finer points of enjoying life will know, if you can top meat with meat, as with a bacon burger; if you can top ice cream with cream, as on a sundae; if you can top vodka with gin for a Martini; and if you can top chocolate cake with chocolate icing, then, my friends, you can definitely fill a braaibroodjie with macaroni and cheese and top it off with more cheese. And, you heretic who's still reading here, I told you to skip to the next page. How can you put tomatoes on your mixed leaves and top that with micro herbs? And how can you add soya milk to tea? The Macaroni and Cheese Braaibroodjie is glorious and needs to be experienced!

WHAT YOU NEED
(makes 6)

12 bread slices
butter
3 litres salted water
250 g macaroni pasta
1 tot white bread or cake flour
1 cup milk
240 g mature Cheddar cheese (grated)
1 tsp Dijon mustard
1 tsp salt
1 tsp black pepper

WHAT TO DO

1. In a big enough potjie over a hot fire, bring 3 litres of water with about half a tot of salt to boiling point. Add all of the macaroni to the bubbling water and cook for exactly 7 minutes. The noodles will still be slightly undercooked, but they will continue cooking later when baking in the sauce. Drain off all water immediately.
2. Return the empty potjie to the fire (not too hot), then add 1 tot of butter and wait until it melts. Add 1 tot of flour and stir for about 1 minute. Now add the milk bit by bit, stirring continuously. You will notice how the butter-and-flour mixture first grows and absorbs all the milk you add, and how this thick paste then starts turning into a sauce as you add more and more milk. If you add the milk too quickly, lumps will form. If at any time you notice lumps forming, first stir them vigorously into the rest of the mixture before adding more milk.
3. When all the milk is in, bring the sauce to a slow simmer and add half of the cheese, as well as all the mustard, salt and pepper, and stir well.
4. Now add the cooked macaroni to the sauce, stir to coat the pasta well, then remove the potjie from the fire and cover with a lid until you assemble the braaibroodjies.
5. Build the braaibroodjies: Spread butter on one side of each slice of bread (these sides will be outward-facing in the assembled braaibroodjie). Pack half these slices buttered-side down and layer with the macaroni mixture and the rest of the cheese. Close the braaibroodjies with the remaining bread slices, buttered sides facing upwards.
6. *'Braaibroodjies is draaibroodjies'*. Braaibroodjies should be turned often and are braaied in a closed, hinged grid. If you don't have one, buy one – preferably with adjustable heights to compress each unit perfectly. You want medium-paced, gentle heat and the grid should be relatively high. Your aim is for the cheese to be melted and all other fillings to be completely heated by the time the outsides are golden brown. Slightly opening and closing your hinged grid a few times after each of the first few turns of the braai process helps the braaibroodjies not to get stuck to the grid.
7. Once done, slice each braaibroodjie in half. Generally, I believe that the correct way to slice braaibroodjies is diagonally and the correct time to serve is immediately.

BAGEL BRAAIBROODJIE

Some people think you can put various toppings on bagels. They are wrong. The only toppings that you should put on bagels are cream cheese, smoked salmon, capers, onion and condiments. The only variation allowed is when you're in South Africa – then it's entirely acceptable (in fact, preferable) to use local salmon trout instead of salmon. Obviously, the more logical bread shape (that is, square and sliced) works perfectly fine, but if you're a traditionalist, the round versions with holes in the middle will lose you some fillings to the coals – but go for it. The way to make a bagel better, because we've already established that you cannot improve it by using other fillings, is to braai it, since it's a well-known fact that everything tastes better when you braai it. Because this is a bagel braaibroodjie, and because you always butter braaibroodjies on the outside, we also butter these braaibroodjies on the outside. When enjoyed before lunchtime, it's entirely acceptable (in fact, encouraged) to enjoy these with a glass of sparkling wine produced in the traditional method – obviously, the superior South African variety (so not Champagne, but MCC).

WHAT YOU NEED
(makes 6)

12 bread slices (or 6 bagels)
butter
plain cream cheese (1 tub will be enough)
100 g smoked salmon trout ribbons or slices (or salmon)
2 tots capers (chopped)
1 red onion (chopped)
salt and freshly ground black pepper
1 lemon

WHAT TO DO

1. Build the braaibroodjies: Spread butter on one side of all of the slices of bread and spread cream cheese on the other sides. Pack half of the slices buttered-side down (and logically, cream-cheese-side up) on a plate or chopping board. Next, you layer the salmon trout ribbons, capers and chopped onions onto the bottom halves. Add salt and pepper then close with the top halves, cream cheese to the inside and butter on top.
2. *'Braaibroodjies is draaibroodjies'*. Braaibroodjie should be turned often and are braaied in a closed, hinged grid. If you don't have one, buy one – preferably with adjustable heights to compress each unit perfectly. You want medium-paced, gentle heat and the grid should be relatively high. In this case, there is no cheese to melt – cream cheese is already soft. As soon as the bread is golden brown on the outside, you're good to go and all other fillings will be somewhat heated by that time.
3. Once done, serve immediately with a wedge of lemon and a glass of sparkling wine.

THE BURGER BRAAIBROODJIE

As the book you are holding in your hands right now rapidly becomes the most-used book in your household, beautiful enough to sit on the coffee table but used so often it mostly hovers between the braai area and kitchen, it will only be a matter of time before the question arises one day in your hovering mind: What to braai tonight – burgers or braaibroodjies? And because braai decisions should never cause you stress, here is a Burger Braaibroodjie for that difficult day of indecision. Solving real-world problems.

WHAT YOU NEED
(makes 4)

8 bread slices
butter or olive oil
500 g good-quality beef mince
chutney
2 tomatoes (sliced)
240 g Cheddar cheese (grated)
1 red onion (thinly sliced)
salt and pepper

WHAT TO DO

1. Use your recently washed hands and divide the beef mince evenly into four heaps. Now use your hands to form your mince into square patties, the best you can. The patties do not have to be perfect – just resembling squares will be good enough.
2. Use a hinged grid and braai the patties over hot coals for 8 minutes until nice and crispy on the outside and medium on the inside. Let the patties rest for a few minutes while you prep the rest of the ingredients.
3. Build the braaibroodjies: Spread butter or olive oil on one side of each slice of bread (these sides will be outward-facing in the assembled braaibroodjie). Pack half these slices buttered-side down then start with a layer of chutney, then the patty, tomato, cheese and onion. If you are autocondimental, also add salt and pepper. Close the braaibroodjies with the remaining bread slices, buttered sides facing upwards.
4. *'Braaibroodjies is draaibroodjies'*. Braaibroodjies should be turned often and are braaied in a closed, hinged grid. If you don't have one, buy one – preferably with adjustable heights to compress each unit perfectly. You want medium-paced, gentle heat and the grid should be relatively high. Your aim is for the cheese to be melted and all other fillings to be completely heated by the time the outsides are golden brown. Slightly opening and closing your hinged grid a few times after each of the first few turns of the braai process helps the braaibroodjies not to get stuck to the grid.
5. Once done, slice each braaibroodjie in half. Generally, I believe that the correct way to slice braaibroodjies is diagonally and the correct time to serve is immediately.

JAN BRAAI LAMB PITA

WHAT YOU NEED
(makes 6)

FOR THE LAMB PITA
6 pita breads
6 lamb leg chops (those big roundish ones)
1 tsp coriander seeds
1 tsp cumin seeds
1 tsp salt
1 tsp ground black pepper
2 garlic cloves (chopped)
1 lemon
1 tot olive oil

FOR THE SAUCE
1 cup Greek yoghurt (or plain yoghurt)
½ cucumber (chopped)
1 tot olive oil
2 garlic cloves (finely chopped)
salt and pepper
lemon juice

FOR THE SALAD FILLING
2 big tomatoes (or 12 cherry tomatoes, chopped)
½ cucumber (the other half)
1 smallish red onion (or half a big one, finely chopped)
1 tot fresh mint
1 tot fresh parsley
1 tot fresh oregano
1 tot olive oil

Depending on whether you prefer speaking Greek, Turkish or Arabic around the braai fire you might also like to call this meal a gyro, döner or shawarma – it's really up to you. Whatever language you speak, the important thing is to gather around a fire. Everyone loves this meal and as a bonus, it looks great in photos. There is no need for a dancing pole with a few revolving tonnes of meat to make a great lamb pita. This is the South African version so we simply braai some chops.

WHAT TO DO

1. Crush the coriander and cumin seeds in a pestle and mortar, and mix in the salt, pepper, garlic cloves, juice from the lemon and olive oil.
2. Rub the chops with the mixture from step 1, cover and let them marinate in a fridge for about 2 hours.
3. Make the sauce by combining the first four ingredients and then adding salt, pepper and a few squeezes of lemon juice to taste.
4. Make the salad by chopping and combining the tomatoes, cucumber, onion, mint, parsley and oregano. Add a bit of olive oil to give it that nice shine.
5. Braai the chops for about 10–12 minutes over hot coals until done.
6. As you remove the chops from the braai, add the pita breads to the grid and toast them for a few minutes, turning a few times and taking extreme care not to let them burn.
7. Use your sharp chef's or carving knife to debone the chops and slice them into thin, diagonal slivers.
8. Open the toasted pita breads and evenly distribute the meat, salad and sauce into them.

BOLOGNESE QUESADILLAS

This recipe can be successfully executed with slices of plain white toasted bread, but if you want to impress your friends, try using wraps.

WHAT YOU NEED
(makes 12)

12 tortilla wraps
500 g good-quality beef mince
1 tot olive oil
1 onion (chopped)
2 garlic cloves (crushed and chopped)
1 chilli (chopped, optional)
1 tot paprika
1 tsp cumin
1 tsp dried coriander
salt and pepper
1 tin or sachet tomato paste (around 50 g)
1 tin chopped tomatoes
1 tin red kidney beans (drained)
1 tsp sugar
240 g Cheddar cheese (sliced or grated)
fresh chillies (optional)

WHAT TO DO

1. Heat the oil in your potjie and fry the onion, garlic and chilli until soft. Add the beef mince and fry until brown and cooked.
2. Season the meat with paprika, cumin, coriander, salt and pepper.
3. Add the tomato paste and let this mix and fry for a few minutes, making sure everything is well mixed together.
4. Next, add your tin of chopped tomatoes and the beans. Add the sugar and let this simmer for 30 minutes on low heat. At the end, give it another taste and season with salt and pepper if needed. Let this cool down slightly.
5. Build your quesadilla: Fill half of the wrap with a layer of Bolognese, then top with Cheddar cheese. Add fresh chillies with the cheese if you are feeling adventurous. Close the wrap, so you now have a half circle. Then fold the wrap again – now you have a quarter circle. Carry on with the rest of the wraps.
6. Carefully arrange the wraps on your hinged grid, and braai over medium coals, turning often. You need to approach them the same way as you would a braaibroodjie.
7. They are ready to serve once the outside is toasted and crisp and the cheese is melted on the inside.

JAN BRAAI PIZZA

This will probably become one of your favourite go-to recipes. It's so simple you might one day even question why it was in a recipe book at all. Whether you are craving it, want to impress guests or are on a road trip and want to do a quick scenic and hassle-free braai, this is a nice trick to have up your sleeve.

I first made this on the *Jan Braai vir Erfenis* television show a few years ago and it went cult overnight. In those first few weeks of the Jan Braai Pizza, many supermarkets sold out of ready-made pizzas on a daily basis, such was the demand. It is widely popular and has been copied, republished and adapted many times over. The possibilities with toppings are endless and you can use whatever your favourite off-the-shelf pizzas are. I usually go for two store-bought pizzas with different toppings and then manually add some extra feta cheese before going to the fire. Enjoy!

WHAT YOU NEED
(feeds 2–4)

2 store-bought pizzas (raw but prepared, with the toppings of your choice)

something extra (including but not limited to feta cheese, garlic, mushrooms, capers, olives, roasted vegetables, sun-dried tomatoes or leftover chopped braaied meat)

a hinged grid

WHAT TO DO

1. Light a fire and wait till the coals are the same heat that you would braai your braaibroodjies on – in other words, medium heat.
2. Place the two pizzas on top of each other with the fillings facing to the inside. If you want to add anything extra, do so beforehand.
3. Place the pizza 'sandwich' in your hinged grid, close the grid tightly and braai the pizza, turning it often, the same as you would do with a braaibroodjie. You want the outside to be toasted and crispy and the cheese on the inside to be completely melted.
4. Once you have achieved the perfect pizza, take it off the grid, slide it onto a wooden board and cut into slices. Serve immediately.

THE ICED-TEA SANDWICH

The British on their muddy island off the west coast of Europe do a soft version of this sandwich and serve it with tea. But here in Africa we know how to make fires and we know how to braai.

WHAT YOU NEED
(makes 6)

12 bread slices
butter
5 big baby marrows (big enough that the slices will not fall through your grid)
good-quality olive oil
freshly ground salt and pepper
a few lemons
1 tub (250 g) **plain cream cheese**
rooibos tea
fruit juice of your choice
ice

WHAT TO DO

1. Use a vegetable peeler to peel the baby marrows into nice thin strips. If you have a well-equipped kitchen and own a mandolin, use that. Once you have peeled all the marrows, place them in a bowl and drizzle with olive oil, then add salt and pepper, and squeeze lemon juice from one of the lemons over them.
2. Now pack the seasoned baby marrow ribbons on your grid and braai over medium coals until they are showing a few char marks. Carefully turn them around. I say 'carefully' as due to their size and texture, they have a tendency to escape the grid and kamikaze it straight into the coals. You definitely only need to turn once and as soon as they have personality, you can take them off.
3. Build the braaibroodjies: Spread butter or olive oil on one side of each slice of bread (these sides will be outward-facing in the assembled braaibroodjie). Pack half these slices buttered-side down and divide and spread the cream cheese onto the non-buttered sides of half of the slices. Top with a layer of braaied baby marrow ribbons. Close the braaibroodjies with the remaining bread slices, buttered sides facing upwards.
4. *Braaibroodjies is draaibroodjies*'. Braaibroodjies should be turned often and are braaied in a closed, hinged grid. If you don't have one, buy one – preferably with adjustable heights to compress each unit perfectly. You want medium-paced, gentle heat and the grid should be relatively high. Your aim is for all the fillings to be completely heated by the time the outsides are golden brown and crisp. Slightly opening and closing your hinged grid a few times after each of the first few turns of the braai process helps the braaibroodjies not to get stuck to the grid.
5. Once done, slice each braaibroodjie in half. Generally, I believe that the correct way to slice braaibroodjies is diagonally and the correct time to serve is immediately.

AND ...

The traditional way is to serve these with iced tea. You prepare that by combining half and half measures of cooled rooibos tea with the fruit juice of your choice and serving that over ice with a slice and squeeze of fresh lemon.

CARAMEL BRAAIBROODJIE

In theory, you could slowly simmer a tin of condensed milk to produce caramel and then use that but in reality, you can just buy a tin of caramel so we are cutting straight to that point. This recipe is inspired by the Argentine alfajor snack and may inspire you to eat caramel shamelessly, at any time of day, just like the people in Argentina. At first, you might wrongly think this is just a dessert braaibroodjie. In actual fact, it can be successfully served for breakfast and also absolutely any other time of the day; for example, in the mid-morning or mid-afternoon with tea.

WHAT YOU NEED
(makes 6)

12 bread slices
butter
1 tin caramel
2 tots desiccated coconut

WHAT TO DO

1. Build the braaibroodjies: Spread butter on one side of each slice of bread (these sides will be outward-facing in the assembled braaibroodjie). Pack half these slices buttered-side down and spread with a layer of caramel. Sprinkle coconut on that. Close the braaibroodjies with the remaining bread slices, buttered sides facing upwards.
2. '*Braaibroodjies is draaibroodjies*'. Braaibroodjies should be turned often and are braaied in a closed, hinged grid. If you don't have one, buy one – preferably with adjustable heights to compress each unit perfectly. You want medium-paced, gentle heat and the grid should be relatively high. Your aim is for the caramel to be completely heated by the time the outsides are golden brown. Slightly opening and closing your hinged grid a few times after each of the first few turns of the braai process helps the braaibroodjies not to get stuck to the grid.
3. Once done, slice each braaibroodjie in half. Generally, I believe that the correct way to slice braaibroodjies is diagonally and the correct time to serve these is immediately, with a cup of tea.

CLASSIC SCONE BRAAIBROODJIE

I am a big fan of fresh scones with whipped cream, strawberry jam and cheese. When I say that I am a big fan of this, I mean that I am a big fan of it being served to me. In my entire life, I've possibly made it for myself once, and if it was even once, I cannot recall that one time. Ordering it, often; making it, never – simply too much effort, as baking cakes and related confectionaries in an oven is not my strong point. However, you can get the same flavours and textures of a fresh scone in your mouth with the scone braaibroodjie. It's actually better. Because it's braaied. So it's crispy yet soft. It's warm, with all the cheese melted, and it's a bit smoky from the fire. And it's easy to make for yourself at home. We've solved the scone problem.

WHAT YOU NEED
(makes 6)

12 bread slices
butter
1 jar strawberry jam
240 g Cheddar cheese (sliced or grated)
250 ml fresh cream (whipped)

WHAT TO DO

1. Build the braaibroodjies: Spread butter on one side of each slice of bread (these sides will be outward-facing in the assembled braaibroodjie). Pack half these slices buttered-side down and spread a generous layer of strawberry jam on each. Top this with a layer of Cheddar cheese. For the scone braaibroodjie, I've yet to pick a favourite between yellow and white Cheddar. They obviously taste the same and I find both equally attractive. Close the braaibroodjies with the remaining bread slices, buttered sides facing upwards.

2. '*Braaibroodjies is draaibroodjies*'. Braaibroodjies should be turned often and are braaied in a closed, hinged grid. If you don't have one, buy one – preferably with adjustable heights to compress each unit perfectly. You want medium-paced, gentle heat and the grid should be relatively high. Your aim is for the cheese to be melted and the jam to be completely heated by the time the outsides are golden brown. Slightly opening and closing your hinged grid a few times after each of the first few turns of the braai process helps the braaibroodjies not to get stuck to the grid.

3. Once done, slice each braaibroodjie in half. Generally, I believe that the correct way to slice braaibroodjies is diagonally and the correct time to serve is immediately. Serve these scone braaibroodjies with freshly whipped cream on top, and naturally in the presence of a cup of tea.

CHOCOLATE BRAAIBROODJIE

The Chocolate Braaibroodjie got its first taste of public acclaim and fame when I made it on the *Jan Braai vir Erfenis* television show quite a few years ago. The day after the show aired, suburban supermarkets had a sudden and unexpected run on sliced white bread and chocolate spread! Fortunately, not everyone reads books at exactly the same time so demand should be more measured now.

WHAT YOU NEED
(makes 6)

12 bread slices
butter
1 jar Nutella or similar chocolate hazelnut spread (you will not use all of it)
100 g slab white chocolate (finely chopped)
50 g pecan nuts (more if you like more, finely chopped)
½ cup sugar
1 tsp cinnamon

WHAT TO DO

1. Build the braaibroodjies: Spread butter on one side of each slice of bread (these sides will be outward-facing in the assembled braaibroodjie). Pack half these slices buttered-side down and spread with a layer of Nutella. Cover the Nutella slices generously with chopped chocolate and pecan nuts. Close the braaibroodjies with the remaining bread slices, buttered sides facing upwards.
2. '*Braaibroodjies is draaibroodjies*'. Braaibroodjies should be turned often and are braaied in a closed, hinged grid. If you don't have one, buy one – preferably with adjustable heights to compress each unit perfectly. You want medium-paced, gentle heat and the grid should be relatively high. Your aim is for the chocolate to be melted by the time the outsides are golden brown. Slightly opening and closing your hinged grid a few times after each of the first few turns of the braai process helps the braaibroodjies not to get stuck to the grid.
3. Just before they are done, mix the sugar and cinnamon together and sprinkle the sugar over the toasted bread. Toast on the fire again on both sides for 1–2 minutes.
4. Once done, slice each braaibroodjie in half. Generally, I believe that the correct way to slice braaibroodjies is diagonally and the correct time to serve is immediately.

WAFFLE BRAAIBROODJIE

Because we can. You do need a waffle machine for this recipe. Well, you, or your loved one. So put a waffle maker on the birthday list of any of the aforementioned individuals.

WHAT YOU NEED
(makes 4)

2 cups white bread or cake flour
½ tot baking powder
½ cup sugar
1 tsp salt
2 eggs
1 cup milk
2 tots butter (roughly, not an exact science – melted)
240 g Cheddar cheese (sliced or grated)
golden syrup

WHAT TO DO

1. Mix the flour, baking powder, sugar and salt together.
2. Mix the eggs, milk and melted butter together, then add to the dry ingredients and mix until smooth.
3. Preheat your waffle machine, spray with non-stick cooking spray and bake the waffles like you would always do or have never done before, until they are cooked and more golden than white on the outside.
4. Once you've baked enough waffles, assemble the waffle braaibroodjie. Distribute the cheese onto half of the waffles and drizzle with syrup. Close the waffle braaibroodjie with the remaining waffles.
5. '*Braaibroodjies is draaibroodjies*'. Approach your waffles the same way you would a braaibroodjie. Braaibroodjies should be turned often and are braaied in a closed, hinged grid. If you don't have one, buy one – preferably with adjustable heights to compress each unit perfectly. You want medium-paced, gentle heat and the grid should be relatively high. Your aim is for the cheese to be melted by the time the outsides are golden brown.
6. Serve immediately as they come off the fire and for bonus points, add a bit of butter on top of each, which will melt into the party.

APPLE TART BRAAIBROODJIE

Apple tart has a golden-brown buttery crust; Apple Tart Braaibroodjie has a golden-brown buttery crust. Apple tart has a set list of regulation ingredients in the filling; Apple Tart Braaibroodjie has the same. Freshly baked apple tart out of the oven is amazing; freshly braaied Apple Tart Braaibroodjie off the fire is also amazing.

WHAT YOU NEED
(makes 6)

12 bread slices
butter
1 tin (400 g) **sliced pie apples**
½ cup raisins
½ tot cinnamon
3 tots brown sugar
250 ml fresh cream (whipped)

WHAT TO DO

1. Build the braaibroodjies: Spread butter on both sides of each slice of bread. Pack half these slices buttered-side down and place apple slices on top. Throw the raisins on top and dust with cinnamon. Add half a tot of sugar to each slice of bread on top of the apples and cinnamon. Close the braaibroodjies with the remaining bread slices, buttered sides facing upwards.
2. '*Braaibroodjies is draaibroodjies*'. Braaibroodjies should be turned often and are braaied in a closed, hinged grid. If you don't have one, buy one – preferably with adjustable heights to compress each unit perfectly. You want medium-paced, gentle heat and the grid should be relatively high. Your aim is for all the fillings to be completely heated by the time the outsides are golden brown. Slightly opening and closing your hinged grid a few times after each of the first few turns of the braai process helps the braaibroodjies not to get stuck to the grid.
3. Once done, slice each braaibroodjie in half. Generally, I believe that the correct way to slice braaibroodjies is diagonally.
4. Add a dollop of fresh cream on top.

MARSHMALLOW AND CHOCOLATE BRAAIBROODJIE

Braaing marshmallows on skewers over some gentle heat is nothing new. I believe it's vital to the braai development of the youth that they do this often, as it teaches them all the fundamentals on how to braai the more tricky items, like – case in point – braaibroodjies, and things like chicken. Gentle heat and turn often. You need the insides cooked before the outside is burnt.

So we know braaied marshmallows are a winner. And I have championed the chocolate braaibroodjie as a dessert of connoisseurs for a few years now. It logically follows that the Marshmallow and Chocolate Braaibroodjie not only works, but works very well. It's a relatively easy braaibroodjie to braai because both marshmallow and chocolate are quite happy to melt quickly, so you're quite likely to have the insides melted by the time the outsides are golden brown. And the bonus: constructing them is very straightforward as well when the crowd is baying for something sweet after a great meal.

WHAT YOU NEED
(makes 6)

12 bread slices
butter
1 packet (150 g) **marshmallows**
2 slabs (100 g each) **chocolate of your choice** (roughly chopped)

WHAT TO DO

1. Cut the marshmallows in half and roughly chop the chocolate.
2. Build the braaibroodjies: Spread butter on one side of each slice of bread (these sides will be outward-facing in the assembled braaibroodjie). Pack half these slices buttered-side down and layer with marshmallow and chocolate. Close the braaibroodjies with the remaining bread slices, buttered sides facing upwards.
3. '*Braaibroodjies is draaibroodjies*'. Braaibroodjies should be turned often and are braaied in a closed, hinged grid. If you don't have one, buy one – preferably with adjustable heights to compress each unit perfectly. You want medium-paced, gentle heat and the grid should be relatively high. Your aim is for the chocolate to be melted and the marshmallows puffed and melted by the time the outsides are golden brown. Slightly opening and closing your hinged grid a few times after each of the first few turns of the braai process helps the braaibroodjies not to get stuck to the grid.
4. Once done, slice each braaibroodjie in half. Generally, I believe that the correct way to slice braaibroodjies is diagonally and the correct time to serve is immediately.

BURGERS

THE BEST AMAZING MUSHROOM BURGER

A burger with a luxuriously creamy cheese-and-mushroom sauce, topped with cheese and mushroom. There is so much fifth element umami flavour in this burger that you'll find a sixth element of flavour if you taste carefully.

WHAT YOU NEED
(makes 4)

FOR THE BURGER

500 g lean beef mince (or 4 high-quality hamburger patties)

4 hamburger rolls

4 big brown mushrooms

olive oil

120 g Cheddar cheese (sliced or grated)

FOR THE SAUCE

1 punnet brown mushrooms

1 onion (chopped)

2 garlic cloves (crushed and chopped)

plain cream cheese (1 tub will be enough)

salt and pepper

WHAT TO DO

1. Convert the 500 g lean beef mince into four equally sized, 100% pure-beef patties. Pure mince binds perfectly for a great patty – don't add anything like onion, breadcrumbs, egg, spices, salt or pepper. Your two recently washed hands are entirely capable of forming patties from mince but a patty press makes the job even easier.
2. Chop all of the brown mushrooms and heat oil in your pan or potjie. Sauté the onion until soft, then add the garlic and chopped mushrooms. Fry until the mushrooms are cooked and have spat out their excess water and that water has started to reduce.
3. Add the cream cheese, stir it in and let this simmer on low heat for a few minutes until thickened. Taste the sauce and add salt and pepper if needed. As with all sauces in this book, if the sauce looks a bit dry or starts to burn, add a bit of water, wine or other suitable liquid.
4. Braai the patties in a grid over very hot coals. Aim for 8 minutes' braai time in total, only turning once. To avoid the patties getting stuck to the grid, you can use a combination of the following tactics: Use a grid with thicker rods; spray the grid with non-stick spray; gently lay the patties onto the grid so that you're not squeezing them into the grid; braai over very hot coals so that the patties seal before sinking into the grid; move the patties slightly with your braai tongs or spatula just as they start to braai and seal, so that ever-so-slightly braaied meat (as opposed to completely raw meat) touches the grid. As the meat cooks, it naturally starts loosening from the grid. Now, only turn the patties once and do that gently.
5. Also braai the big brown mushrooms when you braai the patties. How much you want to braai them is entirely up to you – anything from a little bit of attention to completely soft. Another way to score bonus points is to baste the mushroom with oil during the braai. If you happen to have a bottle of braai sauce in your fridge, you might even baste the mushroom with that during the braai.
6. Oil the insides of the cut rolls and toast on the grid, taking care not to over-toast (burn) them.
7. Assemble the burger: Roll, patty, cheese, mushroom sauce, giant mushroom, roll.

CAPRESE BURGER

Today you don't have to choose between going big or going home because you're already home, having a braai, and with this burger, you are going big. The flavour profile is based on the well-proven success of the margherita pizza and the caprese salad – the tri team of tomatoes, mozzarella cheese and basil.

Now, the quality of ingredients is even more important the simpler the food gets, and in this case, it's no different. You can include the basil component of this burger purely as fresh basil leaves, but this is a burger and burgers like sauce so we are going with basil pesto. Due to the very wide variance in quality of commercially available basil pestos, we're making it ourselves. If you have some trusted local supplier of fresh, high-quality basil pesto, using that is definitely fine; otherwise, just follow the recipe below. When it comes to tomatoes, you need tomatoes that are red in colour – not light coral. This is always the case but especially important today. The mozzarella is quite straightforward, or not. You will pass this exam with the normal mozzarella but you will pass with honours by using buffalo mozzarella, generally sold in brine.

WHAT YOU NEED
(makes 4)

FOR THE BURGER

500 g lean beef mince (or 4 high-quality hamburger patties)

4 hamburger rolls

2 tomatoes (sliced)

1 lemon

olive oil

salt and pepper

120 g mozzarella cheese (more if you like more, sliced or grated)

FOR THE BASIL PESTO

2 punnets (about 40 g) **fresh basil leaves**

2 garlic cloves

2 tots cashew nuts or almonds

4 tots extra-virgin olive oil

salt and pepper

WHAT TO DO

1. Make the pesto: Add all the ingredients together and use a food processor or stick blender to process it. If you like olive oil (like me), add more of it when you feel the urge. Same for all the other ingredients: add more of what you like and less of what you don't like. Taste and add a bit of salt and pepper as needed. You can also use an old-fashioned pestle and mortar to work the ingredients into a paste and make the pesto. If you go this route, chop the basil leaves and garlic quite finely beforehand. Also start with the garlic, basil and some salt to make the grinding process a bit easier.

2. Marinate the tomatoes: Slice the tomatoes and squeeze lemon juice over them. Now drizzle them with olive oil and season with salt and pepper. Let them await their return to the action.

3. Convert the 500 g lean beef mince into four equally sized, 100% pure-beef patties. Pure mince binds perfectly for a great patty – don't add anything like onion, breadcrumbs, egg, spices, salt or pepper. Your two recently washed hands are entirely capable of forming patties from mince but a patty press makes the job even easier.

4. Braai the patties in a grid over very hot coals. Aim for 8 minutes' braai time in total, only turning once. To avoid the patties getting stuck to the grid, you can use a combination of the following tactics: Use a grid with thicker rods; spray the grid with non-stick spray; gently lay the patties onto the grid so that you're not squeezing them into the grid; braai over very hot coals so that the patties seal before sinking into the grid; move the patties slightly with your braai tongs or spatula just as they start to braai and seal, so that ever-so-slightly braaied meat (as opposed to completely raw meat) touches the grid. As the meat cooks, it naturally starts loosening from the grid. Now, only turn the patties once and do that gently.

5. Oil the insides of the cut rolls and toast on the grid, taking care not to over-toast (burn) them. This toasting should be done during the final minute of the patties braaing. Ideally everything should be ready at the same time.

6. Assemble the burger: Roll, patty, cheese, marinated slices of tomato, basil pesto, roll.

MONKEYGLAND BURGER

The globally acclaimed steak and burger sauce from South Africa is the perfect recipe for when you have a few guests over for an extracurricular activity – in other words, if the main action is not the preparation and braaing of food. For example, friends are visiting you to watch a sports game, play some cards or knock back a few sparkling mineral-water cocktails. In such a case, you could prepare the sauce well in advance of their arrival, simply leave it in the pot or pan, and reheat to wake it up for serving. In this scenario, the patties would also be prepared ahead of time, covered and stored in your fridge. When the coals are ready and the time comes to eat, it's simply a matter of braaing the patties and serving the hamburgers. There are already onions and tomatoes in the sauce so no need for that on the roll and on an occasion as described earlier, we can skip the lettuce leaf as well. Kids, interestingly, also really like this one, so logically, as this is a quick and easy process, this meal can also be a trusted go-to on a weeknight at war.

WHAT YOU NEED
(makes 6)

FOR THE BURGER
500 g lean beef mince (or 6 medium-sized high-quality hamburger patties)
6 hamburger rolls (not too big – the cheapest fresh ones at your supermarket)
butter or olive oil

FOR THE SAUCE
1 large onion (finely chopped)
1 tot butter or olive oil
2 garlic cloves (finely chopped)
½ cup tomato sauce
½ cup chutney
3 tots Worcestershire sauce
3 tots water
1 tsp brown sugar
1 tsp vinegar
chilli powder, chilli flakes, fresh chilli or chilli sauce

WHAT TO DO

1. Convert the 500 g lean beef mince into six equally sized, 100% pure-beef patties. Pure mince binds perfectly for a great patty – don't add anything like onion, breadcrumbs, egg, spices, salt or pepper. Your two recently washed hands are entirely capable of forming patties from mince but a patty press makes the job even easier. This is a snack-on-hand or 'street food' style burger – a bit smaller than most of my other recipes in this book – so we're making six patties from the 500 g of mince, as opposed to the four we usually make.
2. Make the sauce: In a pan or pot on the fire or stove, fry the onion in the butter or oil for 4 minutes until golden.
3. Add all the other ingredients, except for the chilli, and simmer for 15 minutes, stirring fairly often to make sure it doesn't burn. If the pot runs dry and the sauce is too thick for your liking, or starts to burn, add a little bit more water.
4. Taste the sauce while it's cooking and if you want to add more bite to it, add a bit of chilli powder, chilli flakes, fresh chilli or a chilli sauce. Don't overdo the chilli – it's supposed to just lift out all the flavours, not dominate the meal.
5. After 15 minutes of simmering, the sauce is ready to serve. You can now keep it warm until the meat is ready.
6. Braai the patties in a grid over very hot coals. Aim for 6 minutes' braai time in total, only turning once. To avoid the patties getting stuck to the grid, you can use a combination of the following tactics: Use a grid with thicker rods; spray the grid with non-stick spray; gently lay the patties onto the grid so that you're not squeezing them into the grid; braai over very hot coals so that the patties seal before sinking into the grid; move the patties slightly with your braai tongs or spatula just as they start to braai and seal, so that ever-so-slightly braaied meat (as opposed to completely raw meat) touches the grid. As the meat cooks, it naturally starts loosening from the grid. Now, only turn the patties once and do that gently.
7. Butter or oil the insides of the cut rolls and toast on the grid, taking care not to over-toast (burn) them.
8. Assemble the burger: Roll, patty, sauce, roll.

FILLET AND BONE MARROW BURGER

When you're feeling flush and want to go full throttle on the opulent life, the logical patty for your hamburger should be a medallion of fillet steak. It's lean, very tender, round (generally in the shape of a patty) and should be braaied over very hot coals to medium-rare perfection. Pretty much the sum of any great hamburger patty, barring the fact that it's almost too lean for a burger. And because of the largesse of the burger at hand, the most obvious topping to adjust the juiciness and flavour is braaied beef bone marrow. The rest of the supporting actors in this play chose themselves.

WHAT YOU NEED
(makes 4)

800 g fillet steak
4 hamburger rolls
olive oil
salt and pepper
4 marrow bone portions (a portion being a lengthwise-halved bone of around 10 cm)
2 tots mayonnaise
1 punnet rocket leaves
2 tomatoes (sliced)
1 lemon
spring onions (chopped)
1 tot Dijon mustard

WHAT TO DO

1. Light a big fire with your favourite braai wood.
2. Cut the steak into four equal pieces and place it on a cutting board, lying sideways. Give each a solid whack or three with a meat mallet or similarly suitable item like a bottle of wine so that each fillet portion is now thinner and has a bigger diameter. Drizzle the meat with olive oil and move around so that all surfaces are coated with oil. Season well with salt and pepper.
3. Now you can braai the steaks over very hot coals for about 8–10 minutes. Make sure you braai the fillets on all sides. A fillet medallion has 4–6 sides and all of them need to face the coals at some time.
4. While you braai the steak, braai the marrow bones too. Season with salt and pepper and braai with the open marrow side facing the coals first until golden brown. Now turn them over, bone side facing the coals, and continue to braai until the marrow starts to bubble or easily comes loose from the bone when encouraged to do so by a spoon or fork.
5. Remove your steak from the fire and let the meat rest.
6. Oil the insides of the cut rolls and toast on the grid, taking care not to over-toast (burn) them.
7. Assemble the burger: Roll, mayonnaise, tomato slices, rocket leaves, fillet steak; then scrape the marrow from the bones onto each steak and spread it all over; put lemon juice on the marrow, then spring onions, mustard on the inside of the top roll, and close it up.

BOBOTIE BURGER

Bobotie is a superstar of South African culinary heritage. The original way to make bobotie is on a fire, obviously, because bobotie was a thing long before electricity was a thing. In this natural evolution of an already-perfect dish, we are not deconstructing, but reconstructing all of the elements of bobotie together into a burger braaied to perfection and served with pride.

WHAT YOU NEED
(makes 4)

FOR THE PATTIES
500 g lean beef mince
1 tot grape vinegar
1 tot apricot jam
1 tot medium curry powder
1 tsp turmeric powder
1 tsp salt
1 tsp pepper

FOR THE BURGER
4 hamburger rolls
butter or olive oil
2 bananas (chopped)
½ cup plain yoghurt
lemon juice
4 eggs (sunny side up)
chutney
2 tomatoes (sliced)
1 onion (sliced)

WHAT TO DO

1. Add all of the vinegar, apricot jam, curry powder, turmeric, salt and pepper together and mix. Now mix this spiced slurry into the mince until there is an equal distribution of spice throughout the mince.
2. Convert the bobotie-spiced mince into four equally sized patties. Your two recently washed hands are entirely capable of forming patties from mince but a patty press makes the job even easier.
3. Prepare the banana sambal by combining the banana and yoghurt and a squeeze of fresh lemon juice. Set aside in your fridge for later.
4. Braai the patties in a grid over hot coals aiming for about 10 minutes' braai time in total and turning about three times in total, so twice to the coals per side. The sugar in the apricot jam, as well as all the spices in the curry that went into the mince, will make these patties more prone to burn than a regular 100% pure-beef patty so we need to braai them over slightly more gentle heat and turn them more often. To avoid the patties getting stuck to the grid, you can use a combination of the following tactics: Use a grid with thicker rods; spray the grid with non-stick spray; gently lay the patties onto the grid so that you're not squeezing them into the grid; move the patties slightly with your braai tongs or spatula just as they start to braai and seal, so that ever-so-slightly braaied meat (as opposed to completely raw meat) touches the grid. As the meat cooks, it naturally starts loosening from the grid. Now turn the patties, and do that gently.
5. Butter or oil the insides of the cut rolls and toast on the grid, taking care not to over-toast (burn) them.
6. During the very final stages of the braai, multitask or get your braai assistant to fry the four eggs sunny side up so that they are just perfectly fried and still warm and soft for the assembly of the burger.
7. Assemble the burger: Roll, banana sambal, patty, chutney, tomato, onion, fried egg, roll.

MADAGASCAN PEPPERCORN BURGER

This one, as the name suggests, comes from the island in the Indian Ocean where I've had the privilege of spending some quality time. On this very unique part of earth, in both the more formal food markets, as well as at street vendor stalls, you can find a variety of repurposed bottles and jars, filled to the brim with beautiful green peppercorns in brine. The trick to making this peppercorn sauce is locating such green peppercorns back home in your local supermarket. Back home, they are sold in small glass jars and are usually hidden away on a shelf somewhere in the general vicinity of the olives. The rest of the ingredients are straightforward to find in a supermarket.

Note that while a burger patty will work, I make my Madagascan Peppercorn Burger with thinly sliced steak – sliced thinly after being braaied, not before. Beef in Madagascar comes from the Zebu cow, quite a tough animal, medium sized and adapted to tropical climates. It's used for farming practices (as in pulling stuff), and it's milked and also produces beef to eat. As you might imagine, the Zebu is mostly pasture-reared and all of this combines to give you beef meat with quite a distinctive flavour, but also meat that is quite tough – the type of steak I believe you slice into very thin slivers with your most-prized championship knife before serving it to your guests. And whilst I suggest you make this burger with a great South African beef steak, I still do thin slices of that steak to pay homage to the Zebu cattle of Madagascar.

WHAT YOU NEED
(makes 4)

FOR THE BURGER
800 g rump steak
4 hamburger rolls
butter or olive oil
lettuce
2 tomatoes (sliced)
1 onion (sliced)
salt and black pepper

FOR THE SAUCE
1 tot butter
1 tot white bread or cake flour
1 tub (250 ml) **cream**
1 small jar green peppercorns (about 2–3 tots when drained)
1 tot Dijon mustard
1 tot brandy (optional)
salt and black pepper

WHAT TO DO

1. Light a big fire and while you wait for the wood to convert to coals through an ancient and very natural process, prepare, measure and arrange all of the ingredients. You will have to braai the steak and make the sauce simultaneously, which is entirely possible. That's just how this recipe works.
2. Make the pepper sauce: Melt the butter in a pot or pan on the fire or stove then add the flour and mix well. Immediately start adding a little bit of cream at a time and stir continuously. Keep on adding the cream until it is all in and the sauce is smooth. Drain the peppercorns and add them. Also add the mustard and brandy and stir that in (if you don't like brandy in your sauce, don't add brandy to the sauce). Now let the sauce simmer until you are happy with the consistency, then season with salt and black pepper.
3. Braai the steak or steaks over very hot coals for 8 minutes in total until they are medium rare. You can season the meat just before, during or after the braai, depending on when you believe it's best to season meat. As you might guess, I don't think it matters when you salt the steak, because it won't make any noticeable difference to the end result of this meal. You only need to turn the steaks once, which is a good thing – you can focus the bulk of your attention on perfecting the pepper sauce.
4. The steak needs to rest before you slice it. This should be for at least 5 minutes so use this time to finish making the sauce. When you slice the steak, lie it flat on a cutting board and go in at a 45-degree angle instead of straight down. This allows you to slice through the fibres in the meat an additional time, resulting in even more tender slices of meat. If you struggle to produce neat, thin slices, you need to sharpen your chef's or carving knife, or you need a new knife altogether.
5. Butter or oil the insides of the cut rolls and toast on the grid, taking care not to over-toast (burn) them.
6. Assemble the burger: Roll, lettuce, tomato, onion, steak slices, sauce, roll.

NACHO BURGER

To be honest, the origin of this recipe is looks. I constructed it first because I thought that it would look very nice on a photo, and considering that half of this book is photos, having a burger that performs very well in the looks department wasn't going to hurt. But as we all know, food that looks great also tastes better. And in this case the Nacho Burger certainly does not disappoint: it scores high in appearance and coincidentally, also performs very well on all the taste buds in your mouth. We have a wide variety of complementing flavours, and the nacho chips deliver a beautiful crunch and broaden the range of textures in this meal.

WHAT YOU NEED
(makes 4)

500 g good-quality lean beef mince (or 4 high-quality hamburger patties)
4 hamburger rolls
2 avocados
salt and pepper
1 lemon
2 tomatoes (chopped into small blocks)
1 red onion (finely chopped)
1 small chilli (chopped, optional)
fresh coriander leaves (a bunch, chopped)
2 whole mielies (corn)
sour cream
120 g Cheddar cheese (grated)
1 pack tortilla chips or corn chips (something like Doritos)

WHAT TO DO

1. Convert the 500 g lean beef mince into four equally sized, 100% pure-beef patties. Pure mince binds perfectly for a great patty – don't add anything like onion, breadcrumbs, egg, spices, salt or pepper. Your two recently washed hands are entirely capable of forming patties from mince but a patty press makes the job even easier.
2. Make the guacamole: Mash the avocado with a fork, season with salt, pepper and lemon juice.
3. Make most of the salsa: Chop the tomatoes into small blocks, add the chopped onion and chopped chilli. Do not overdo the chilli – it's there to lift out flavours, not to punish or torment your guests. Season with salt, pepper and lastly mix the freshly chopped coriander leaves in.
4. Braai the mielies on a braai grid at the same time as the patties, and grill on all sides. Braaied mielies have significantly more flavour than non-braaied mielies. Once charred a bit, remove from the fire and use a sharp knife to cut the kernels off the cob. Add the charred mielie kernels to the rest of the salsa and mix.
5. Braai the patties in a grid over very hot coals. Aim for 8 minutes' braai time in total, only turning once. To avoid the patties getting stuck to the grid, you can use a combination of the following tactics: Use a grid with thicker rods; spray the grid with non-stick spray; gently lay the patties onto the grid so that you're not squeezing them into the grid; braai over very hot coals so that the patties seal before sinking into the grid; move the patties slightly with your braai tongs or spatula just as they start to braai and seal, so that ever-so-slightly braaied meat (as opposed to completely raw meat) touches the grid. As the meat cooks, it naturally starts loosening from the grid. Now, only turn the patties once and do that gently. After the patties are turned, during the last few minutes of the braai, add the cheese on top so that the heat of the fire and patties can melt it.
6. Cut your rolls in half and toast on the grid, taking care not to over-toast (burn) them.
7. Assemble the burger: Roll, sour cream, guacamole, patty with cheese, salsa, nacho chips; lastly, spread sour cream on the inside of the top half of the roll and close it up.

STEAK PREGO ROLL

Considering how awesome it tastes, this is a very straightforward recipe and I suggest you simply learn it off by heart. It will save you a lot of time and effort as in future, you won't need to find a Portuguese restaurant every time you crave a steak prego roll. The peri-peri sauce you mix for this recipe and use as a marinade, as well as serving sauce, is more than you will need for this recipe. Keep what you don't use in your fridge and deploy it as a marinade, basting or serving sauce with any braaied food over the upcoming days.

WHAT YOU NEED
(makes 4)

FOR THE PREGO ROLLS

800 g rump or sirloin steak (buy 1 or 2 rump or sirloin steaks and slice them into 4 roughly equally sized portions)

4 hamburger rolls (preferably Portuguese rolls)

butter or olive oil

lettuce

2 tomatoes (sliced)

FOR THE SAUCE

8 garlic cloves (crushed and finely chopped)

½ cup olive oil

½ cup grape vinegar (red or white)

½ cup lemon juice

½ cup water

1 tot paprika

1 tot chilli powder

1 tot salt

a few small hot chillies (piri-piri/African bird's eye, finely chopped)

WHAT TO DO

1. Throw the finely chopped garlic into a glass bottle or jar with the oil, grape vinegar, lemon juice, water, paprika, chilli powder and salt. Shake well until the ingredients are mixed and all the salt dissolved.
2. Now taste the sauce and if you want it hotter, add a few finely chopped fresh chillies to the sauce, and shake. You can add as many chillies as you wish but remember that you can never expect your guests to eat a sauce that is too hot for them. If, like me, you like quite a lot of burn, then it might be wise to mix two batches – one hot and one with fewer chillies.
3. Do not touch your eyes or any other sensitive parts of your body while you are making this sauce as the traces of chilli juice left on your hands will burn those sensitive parts. Go and wash your hands to get the chilli juices off them, and then still be careful.
4. Pound each steak with a meat mallet to make it tender and better able to absorb the marinade. As you will eat the steak straight from the roll, you want it nice and soft so the average set of teeth can bite clean through it.
5. Place the steaks in a marinating bowl and pour some, not all, of the peri-peri sauce over them. Flip them over using a tool like a spoon and get some sauce on the other sides of the steaks as well. You want to coat both sides of each steak, but it is not necessary for the steaks to swim in the sauce so there will be leftover sauce, which can be used for dressing the rolls later and for absolutely anything else in the following days. To be clear, you will keep the leftover sauce not used as marinade. Whatever sauce you used as marinade was in touch with raw meat and will need to be discarded.
6. Cover the bowl of marinating steaks and place in a cool place like a fridge. Go and light the fire.
7. When the coals are ready, and they must be hot to very hot, braai the steaks until medium rare. For a thin 200 g steak, this could take about 5 minutes but definitely not more than 8 minutes.
8. Butter or oil the insides of the cut rolls and toast on the grid, taking care not to over-toast (burn) them.
9. Assemble the burger: Roll, lettuce, tomato, steak, roll. Let your guests add extra peri-peri sauce until their prego is as hot and drenched as they like it.

THE BIG BURGER

You only live once and might as well go full throttle. This is a single-serving burger, for special people on special occasions. We're converting half a kilogram of pure-beef mince into four bespoke hamburger patties. They are sealed on a grid over very hot coals and then basted on both sides. Cheese goes onto each hot patty as they come off the fire (in this case, we're going for the highest-quality processed Cheddar-flavoured cheese spread you can find), ensuring maximum flavour and increased melting. An entirely epic ultimate braai tower of power.

WHAT YOU NEED
(makes 1)

500 g lean beef mince
1 hamburger roll (a relatively substantial one)
2 tots tomato sauce
2 tots chutney
1 tot Worcestershire sauce
butter or olive oil
lettuce
1 tomato (sliced)
1 onion (sliced)
Cheddar cheese spread
1 skewer

WHAT TO DO

1. Convert the 500 g lean beef mince into four equally sized, 100% pure-beef patties. Pure mince binds perfectly for a great patty – don't add anything like onion, breadcrumbs, egg, spices, salt or pepper. Your two recently washed hands are entirely capable of forming patties from mince but a patty press makes the job even easier. To be clear, all four of these patties will go onto the same burger. We're doing homemade patties because you need the slight imperfection of it for the character of this burger. As you want the stack to hold up, err on the side of a patty with larger diameter as opposed to a thicker one.
2. Make the basting by mixing the tomato sauce, chutney and Worcestershire sauce.
3. Braai the patties in a grid over very hot coals. Aim for 8 minutes' braai time in total. In this case, you want to baste the patties with the sauce during the braai and after the final turn, while handling and turning the patties as little as possible. Logically, this means gently laying the patties on the grid (don't press them into the grid and let them get stuck). After about 3 minutes, you turn and baste. After another 3 minutes, you turn and baste. A minute later, as the basted side now facing the coals starts to sizzle, you turn a final time. As soon as the basting on the side now facing the coals starts to sizzle, remove from the fire and build the burger.
4. Butter or oil the insides of the cut roll and toast on the grid during the last minute or two of the patties being braaied, taking care not to over-toast (burn) them.
5. Assemble the burger: Roll, lettuce, tomato, onion, patty, cheese spread, patty, cheese spread, patty, cheese spread, patty, cheese spread, onion, tomato, lettuce, roll. If things are getting out of control use a skewer straight down the middle to provide some backbone. (The skewer-as-backbone solution works well with spineless burghers, but is unfortunately not practical with politicians).

CHEESE AND BACON BURGER

I don't think there is any single, definitive set of burger toppings but some, like cheese and bacon, are certainly more popular than others. I went through a phase of my life when I never made any burger other than the one in the recipe below. The flavour of your cheese sauce depends directly on the quality and taste of the cheese you use, obviously. The better-tasting the cheese, the better-tasting the sauce. Quantity- and quality-wise, err on the side of extravagance. I often use a mixture of Cheddar, Parmesan and whatever else happens to be in my fridge. I believe, in this case, that the bacon should be streaky and crisp. You get it crisp by braaing it on a grid over the coals of your fire.

Now, I know that burgers topped with bacon and cheese (not cheese sauce such as in this case – just normal cheese) are commercially quite a thing but that is simply not nearly as good as this number. This is the real deal.

WHAT YOU NEED
(makes 4)

500 g lean beef mince (or 4 high-quality hamburger patties)
4 hamburger rolls
butter
1 tot white bread or cake flour
1 cup milk (full cream, obviously)
1 tot Dijon mustard
1 cup grated cheese (not an exact science but anything from about 120–150 g will be fine)
salt and black pepper
1 packet bacon
lettuce
2 large tomatoes (sliced)

WHAT TO DO

1. Convert the 500 g lean beef mince into four equally sized, 100% pure-beef patties. Pure mince binds perfectly for a great patty – don't add anything like onion, breadcrumbs, egg, spices, salt or pepper. Your two recently washed hands are entirely capable of forming patties from mince but a patty press makes the job even easier.
2. Make the sauce: Melt 1 tot of butter in a pot over medium heat and then add the 1 tot of flour. Stir until the flour is mixed smoothly with the butter, and then cook for 1 minute, stirring all the time.
3. Pour in the milk bit by bit while stirring vigorously to incorporate it completely and make a smooth sauce. A wooden spoon should work fine, but if you struggle, use a metal hand whisk. Never leave the sauce unattended; believe me, I speak from experience. If at any time you feel you're losing control, decrease the amount of heat reaching the pot and first fully combine everything already in the pot before adding more milk.
4. As soon as all the milk has been incorporated, toss in the mustard and cheese. Stir well until the cheese has melted.
5. Take the pot off the heat and test for seasoning. Add salt and pepper if the sauce needs it. Some cheeses are very salty already and the sauce will only need a decent grinding of black pepper. Keep the sauce aside until the burgers are ready. Reheat and stir just before pouring it over the burgers – and don't worry about that 'skin' forming on top of the sauce, for it stirs away. Alternatively, make the sauce while braaing the patties.
6. Braai the patties in a grid over very hot coals. Aim for 8 minutes' braai time in total, only turning once.
7. Bacon must be cooked crispy. The easiest and tastiest way to achieve this is on a braai grid over the coals. Lay the pieces out carefully, so that they don't fall through the grid, and only turn them once on the braai. If there's space on your grid, do this at the same time that you're braaing the patties. Remove from the fire when ready.
8. Butter the insides of the cut rolls and toast on the grid, taking care not to over-toast (burn) them.
9. Assemble the burger: Roll, lettuce, tomato, bacon, patty, cheese sauce, roll.

THE STOUT BEER BURGER

To experience the joy of this flavour combination, you can travel all the way to Ireland, sit in a pub and order a pie. Or you could simply head to your nearest South African fire and have a braai!

WHAT YOU NEED
(makes 4)

500 g lean beef mince (or 4 high-quality hamburger patties)
4 hamburger rolls
butter or olive oil
1 onion (sliced)
1 punnet mushrooms (chopped)
1 cup stout beer
1 block beef stock (or 2 tsp beef stock powder)
½ tsp black pepper

WHAT TO DO

1. Convert the 500 g lean beef mince into four equally sized, 100% pure-beef patties. Pure mince binds perfectly for a great patty – don't add anything like onion, breadcrumbs, egg, spices, salt or pepper. Your two recently washed hands are entirely capable of forming patties from mince but a patty press makes the job even easier.
2. Heat the oil or butter in a pan and fry the onion and mushrooms until soft. Add the beer, beef stock cube (or powder) and pepper and simmer for 10 minutes or more until most of the liquid is gone, the onions look nicely caramelised and the mushrooms cooked.
3. Braai the patties in a grid over very hot coals. Aim for 8 minutes' braai time in total, only turning once. To avoid the patties getting stuck to the grid, you can use a combination of the following tactics: Use a grid with thicker rods; spray the grid with non-stick spray; gently lay the patties onto the grid so that you're not squeezing them into the grid; braai over very hot coals so that the patties seal before sinking into the grid; move the patties slightly with your braai tongs or spatula just as they start to braai and seal, so that ever-so-slightly braaied meat (as opposed to completely raw meat) touches the grid. As the meat cooks, it naturally starts loosening from the grid. Now, only turn the patties once and do that gently.
4. Butter or oil the sliced rolls and toast on the grid, taking care not to over-toast (burn) them.
5. Assemble the burger: Roll, onion and mushrooms, patty, onion and mushrooms, roll.

STEAK SANDWICH WITH MUSTARD, MAYO AND CARAMELISED ONIONS

People who know me know that I don't believe the only way to serve steak is in one massive and intimidating piece on a plate. Braaing a great steak can also be seen as the first step to creating something like an awesome steak sandwich. Caramelised onions are the other special part of this sandwich. Although made from the same core ingredient and similar in appearance, do not confuse caramelised onions with fried onions. The former are much sweeter, owing to the longer cooking time, which gives the sugars in the onion more time to caramelise, and the flavour more time to develop. It's a good idea to make the caramelised onions ahead of your braai, leaving you time to focus on braaing the steak to perfection.

WHAT YOU NEED
(makes 4)

800 g rump or sirloin steak (steak is usually not sold in exact weights, so buy enough steak that you have a total weight of around 800 g)
8 bread slices (fresh, good-quality bread of your choice, or 4 quality rolls)
butter or olive oil
4 onions (finely sliced into rings or long strips, not diced)
3 tots brown sugar
2 tots balsamic vinegar
salt and black pepper
2 tots Dijon mustard
lettuce (washed)
4 tots mayonnaise (creamy)

WHAT TO DO

1. In a pot or pan over medium heat (not too hot), heat a generous amount of olive oil or butter and add the sliced onions. Fry gently until they become soft, then continue to fry gently until they begin to turn brown and slightly caramelised from their natural sugars. This should take about 20 minutes – be patient!
2. Now add the brown sugar and vinegar and keep stirring. Cook for another 5–10 minutes, stirring often, until the liquid becomes reduced and syrupy. Season lightly with salt and pepper (the flavours are already quite intense, so not a lot), stir well and remove from the heat. Cover and store the onions where flies can't attack them. You can cook the onions in advance before your guests arrive. Caramelised onions keep well in the fridge for a few days.
3. Braai the steak or steaks over very hot coals for 8 minutes in total until they are medium rare. You can season the meat just before, during or after the braai, depending on when you believe it's best to season meat. As you might guess, I don't think it matters when you salt the steak, because it won't make any noticeable difference to the end result of this meal.
4. The steaks need to rest before you slice them. This should be for at least 5 minutes, but can be for a few hours as well, as it's entirely acceptable to use cold steak for this sandwich. When you slice the steaks, lie them flat on a cutting board and go in at a 45-degree angle instead of straight down. This allows you to slice through the fibres in the meat an additional time, resulting in even more tender slices of meat. If you struggle to produce neat, thin slices, you need to sharpen your chef's or carving knife, or you need a new knife altogether.
5. Butter or oil the slices of bread and toast on the grid, taking care not to over-toast (burn) them.
6. Assemble the sandwich: Bread, mustard, lettuce, steak strips, caramelised onion, mayonnaise on the other slice of bread, bread.

HAND-CHOPPED BURGER

In my experience, the juiciness, texture and flavour of a burger patty made with homemade, hand-chopped mince means you need slightly more of it. People (you and me included) tend to eat more of the food the nicer it is. So, whereas most other beef burger recipes in this book call for 500 g of meat (which equates to four patties of 125 g each), we're going for at least 600 g here, leading to patties of at least 150 g each.

Roughly half of your meat should be from the forequarter and the other half from the hindquarter. The former is tougher, has more fat and flavour, and the latter is leaner and more tender, giving you a balanced overall mince and resultant patty. Various other cuts work but from a practical point of view, this means that to make four burgers, I buy roughly 400 g of chuck steak and a single supermarket portion of rump or sirloin for the balance, to get to a total weight of just over 700 g. Chuck steaks usually contain bones so you're still going to lose that weight.

Hand-chopping a steak into mince doesn't really need to be an overly aggressive process involving a large cleaver – a solid and sharp chef's knife will do the trick. Wooden chopping boards are more photogenic but plastic makes more sense here if you're an aggressive chopper with a cleaver – we want chopped meat, not chopped wood in the patty. When converting steak into mince by chopping it by hand, you want the meat as cold as possible. It works best to put the steaks in a freezer for an hour or two before you start. Just don't go all Arctic on them – the meat should not reach frozen.

On the chopping board, step one is to debone the chuck and to discard the bones. Now, slice all the meat into thin slivers, as you would when serving braaied steak. Yet again, slice each sliver lying flat into strips (you can stack a few at a time), leaving you with very thin strips resembling julienned vegetables. Change direction by 90 degrees and slice or chop everything into many little non-identical pieces. Beauty here lies in the imperfection.

Don't add anything to the mince. After all, you're eating 100% pure steak – you've just rearranged its shape: the fat strips have been minced or chopped up and spread evenly inside the meat; there are no tough bits in the steak, and it has a uniform shape, which will braai more evenly. That's also why I believe you should braai homemade burger patties medium rare – exactly like a steak.

WHAT YOU NEED
(makes 4)

FOR THE BURGER
350 g sirloin or rump steak
400 g chuck steak
4 hamburger rolls
sea salt
butter or olive oil
lettuce
tomato (sliced)

FOR THE SAUCE
½ cup mayonnaise (creamy)
1 tot tomato sauce
1 tot Dijon mustard
1 gherkin (normal-sized, chopped)
1 tsp garlic powder
1 tsp paprika
½ tsp cayenne pepper

WHAT TO DO

1. Make the sauce by adding all the ingredients to a bowl and blending with your stick blender, or a strong arm and whisk, until smooth. Alternatively, add all of the ingredients to a food processor and process until smooth.
2. Convert the steak into mince by means of a chopping board and a sharp chef's knife or cleaver. If you don't own a sharp chef's knife, buy one – and also buy a knife sharpener.
3. When you have all your hand-chopped mince ready, shape it into four 100% pure-beef, hand-chopped burger patties using your hands or a patty press. Don't add anything to the mince – we're busy with high-level, classy stuff; we're not making meatballs.
4. Carefully lay the patties down on an open grid over very hot coals and braai for 8 minutes in total, only turning them once. During the braai you can put pure sea salt on both sides of the patties.
5. During the final few minutes of the braai, cut and butter the rolls, and toast the insides over the coals.
6. Assemble the burger: Roll, lettuce, tomato, patty, burger sauce, roll.

MUSTARD AND CAPER BURGER

Within my closer circle of relatives and friends, this one is very popular. I don't think it's because they have a particular quirk but rather because this is simply very tasty, so if you're looking to overperform with little effort, this is the recipe to use.

Like absolutely every recipe in this book, the exact taste will depend on the quality of the ingredients that you use, and in this case, also on your choices of mustard. I suggest that you use half Dijon and half wholegrain but by all means, experiment with using a different combination of mustards and find the potion you like best. But for guests, do be wary of a heavy hand on hot English mustard, which isn't everyone's cup of tea.

WHAT YOU NEED
(makes 4)

FOR THE BURGER
500 g lean beef mince
(or 4 high-quality hamburger patties)
4 hamburger rolls
butter or olive oil
lettuce
2 tomatoes (sliced)
1 onion (sliced)

FOR THE MUSTARD SAUCE
1 tot butter
1 tot white bread or cake flour
½ cup white wine
½ cup milk
2 tots Dijon mustard
2 tots wholegrain mustard
1 tot capers
salt and pepper

WHAT TO DO

1. Convert the 500 g lean beef mince into four equally sized, 100% pure-beef patties. Pure mince binds perfectly for a great patty – don't add anything like onion, breadcrumbs, egg, spices, salt or pepper. Your two recently washed hands are entirely capable of forming patties from mince but a patty press makes the job even easier.
2. Make the sauce: In a pan or pot, melt the butter and then add the flour. Mix the two vigorously and as it forms a paste, start adding the wine. Continue stirring vigorously until all the wine is in. Now add the milk bit by bit, continuously stirring. Once all the milk is in, add the mustard and capers, and stir. Sample the sauce, and add salt and pepper to taste. How you want to play this is to let the sauce simmer very gently while you braai the patties, and until you are happy with the consistency.
3. Braai the patties in a grid over very hot coals. Aim for 8 minutes' braai time in total, only turning once. To avoid the patties getting stuck to the grid, you can use a combination of the following tactics: Use a grid with thicker rods; spray the grid with non-stick spray; gently lay the patties onto the grid so that you're not squeezing them into the grid; braai over very hot coals so that the patties seal before sinking into the grid; move the patties slightly with your braai tongs or spatula just as they start to braai and seal, so that ever-so-slightly braaied meat (as opposed to completely raw meat) touches the grid. As the meat cooks, it naturally starts loosening from the grid. Now, only turn the patties once and do that gently.
4. Butter or oil the insides of the cut rolls and toast on the grid, taking care not to over-toast (burn) them.
5. Assemble the burger: Roll, lettuce, tomato, onion, patty, mustard sauce, roll.

AND ...

If you have leftover capers after making this recipe, consider using them in the Chicken Caesar Burger (page 196) over the next few days.

BRAAI FREEDOM FIGHTER

The Braai Freedom Fighter does not play games. It's a robust burger with little interest in debate, and it dominates your plate. You use 100% pure red meat to make the burger patties, and the sauce is made with the finest red ingredients known to braai kind – significant figureheads like red onions, red bell peppers, paprika, cayenne pepper and tomato. Even the stock we use to bring it all together is beef stock, from a red-blooded, 100% red-meat animal. If the ferocity of the Braai Freedom Fighter scares you, enjoy it with a dollop of fresh sour cream, as the two complement each other very well.

WHAT YOU NEED
(makes 4)

500 g lean beef mince (or 4 high-quality hamburger patties)
4 hamburger rolls
olive oil
2 red onions (sliced or chopped)
2 red bell peppers (seeded and chopped)
2 garlic cloves (crushed and chopped)
1 tsp chilli powder (or cayenne pepper)
2 tots paprika
2 tomatoes (chopped)
1 tot tomato paste
½ cup beef stock
salt and pepper
sour cream (a 250 ml tub is more than enough)
parsley

WHAT TO DO

1. Convert the 500 g lean beef mince into four equally sized, 100% pure-beef patties. Pure mince binds perfectly for a great patty – don't add anything like onion, breadcrumbs, egg, spices, salt or pepper. Your two recently washed hands are entirely capable of forming patties from mince but a patty press makes the job even easier.
2. Start making the sauce by heating olive oil in a potjie and frying the onions and peppers for a few minutes until they start to soften, then throw in the garlic. Onions take longer to cook than garlic, so always fry onions before adding any garlic. This is general advice and is not only applicable to this recipe.
3. Add the chilli powder and paprika, and toss to release their flavours. Then also add the tomatoes, tomato paste and beef stock, and mix to combine them all. Bring to the boil, close the lid and simmer until you start to braai the patties. Basically you want to let it simmer so that the flavour can develop while the fire burns down and you can start to braai. Check every now and then to stir the potjie and make sure it doesn't cook dry. You want the sauce to thicken but you don't want it to burn. When you start braaing the patties, take the lid off the sauce and let it reduce to your liking, adding extra heat under the potjie if necessary to get it reduced more rapidly. During this time, also sample the sauce and add salt and pepper to taste.
4. Braai the patties in a grid over very hot coals. Aim for 8 minutes' braai time in total, only turning once. To avoid the patties getting stuck to the grid, you can use a combination of the following tactics: Use a grid with thicker rods; spray the grid with non-stick spray; gently lay the patties onto the grid so that you're not squeezing them into the grid; braai over very hot coals so that the patties seal before sinking into the grid; move the patties slightly with your braai tongs or spatula just as they start to braai and seal, so that ever-so-slightly braaied meat (as opposed to completely raw meat) touches the grid. As the meat cooks, it naturally starts loosening from the grid. Now, only turn the patties once and do that gently.
5. Oil the sliced rolls and toast on the grid, taking care not to over-toast (burn) them.
6. Assemble the burger: Roll, patty, Braai Freedom Fighter sauce, dollop sour cream, chopped parsley, roll.

CHIMICHURRI STEAK ROLL

As you would hope, I have a few strong views on braai-related matters. You would hope that the views are strongly held because penning views you're not really sure of in a published book would be a silly thing to do. With steak being a very popular and regularly braaied item, I have naturally developed some opinions on that as well. Regulation portions of steak are usually sold with a thickness of about 2½ cm. I believe these types of steaks should be braaied over very hot coals for about 8 minutes in total. You only need to turn them once during the braai and it doesn't really matter if you salt them just before, during or after the braai. They are best enjoyed medium rare and you're aiming for a final maximum temperature of 52 °C in the middle of the thickest part.

Furthermore, I do not like to serve or be served such a steak in a single piece. I like to carve steaks into thin slivers with the best and sharpest chef's knife on hand, serving the steak in slices. My view is that this makes eating it more pleasant for all present, as opposed to having half a cow carcass on your plate and having to dissect that with a blunt steak knife that really should have retired at the end of last season.

When serving steak in the manner that I prefer, two dressings tower above all: these are either garlic butter, which then melts from the heat of the steak, or chimichurri sauce. When going for chimichurri sauce, follow this recipe (which is completely foolproof) and serve it in a fresh bread roll for a full and balanced meal!

WHAT YOU NEED
(makes 4)

FOR THE BURGER
800 g rump or sirloin steak (steak is usually not sold in exact weights – buy enough steak so that you have a total weight of around 800 g)
4 hamburger rolls
salt and pepper
butter or olive oil

FOR THE CHIMICHURRI SAUCE
4 long red chillies (deseeded and chopped)
4 long green chillies (deseeded and chopped)
2 garlic cloves (crushed and chopped)
½ tot dried oregano
1 tsp coarse ground salt
1 tsp ground black pepper
1 tot white wine vinegar
2 tots olive oil
½ cup flat leaf parsley

WHAT TO DO

1. Prepare the sauce: Grab your stick blender or food processor (or if there's loadshedding, your pestle and mortar) and convert all of the ingredients for the sauce into exactly that: a sauce.
2. Braai the steak or steaks over very hot coals for 8 minutes in total until they are medium rare. You can season the meat just before, during or after the braai, depending on when you believe it's best to season meat. As you might guess, I don't think it matters when you salt the steak, because it won't make any noticeable difference to the end result of this meal.
3. The steaks need to rest before you slice them. This should be for at least 5 minutes, but can be for a few hours as well, as it's entirely acceptable to use cold steak for this roll. When you slice the steaks, lie them flat on a cutting board and go in at a 45-degree angle instead of straight down. This allows you to slice through the fibres in the meat an additional time, resulting in even more tender slices of meat. If you struggle to produce neat, thin slices, you need to sharpen your chef's or carving knife, or you need a new knife altogether.
4. Butter or oil the rolls and toast on the grid, taking care not to over-toast (burn) them.
5. Assemble: Roll, steak strips, sauce, roll.

BACON, PINEAPPLE AND SWEET-CHILLI BURGER

This recipe started out when my parents had a particularly large crop of chillies in their herb garden. You can only use that many chillies in your curry potjies and so we decided to try and make sweet-chilli sauce with some of the red devils. Practice makes perfect and before long there was the sweet-chilli sauce recipe below, which as you will see once you make it, is very good! I feel that a properly braaied beef burger is the perfect vehicle to carry this sauce to your mouth, and that braaied bacon and pineapple are the best fellow passengers the sauce could possibly wish for.

WHAT YOU NEED
(makes 4)

500 g lean beef mince (or 4 high-quality hamburger patties)
4 hamburger rolls
5 chillies (any type or a combination, with a few extra on standby)
2 garlic cloves (crushed or chopped)
½ cup apple cider vinegar (or rice vinegar or white grape vinegar)
½ cup water
½ cup sugar
1 tsp salt
1 tsp soy sauce
½ tot cornflour mixed with ½ tot water
1 packet bacon
1 pineapple (peeled and sliced into rings)
butter or olive oil
lettuce
tomato (sliced)
1 cup mozzarella cheese (grated)

WHAT TO DO

1. Convert the 500 g lean beef mince into four equally sized, 100% pure-beef patties. Pure mince binds perfectly for a great patty – don't add anything like onion, breadcrumbs, egg, spices, salt or pepper. Your two recently washed hands are entirely capable of forming patties from mince but a patty press makes the job even easier.
2. Make the sauce: Chop the chillies finely. If you don't want too much burn in the sauce, remove some or all of the seeds. If you like it hot, leave the seeds in. If you think the chillies you have are quite mild, use more than 5 chillies. If you think the chillies you have are particularly potent, use your common sense and good luck!
3. Throw the chopped chillies, garlic, vinegar, water, sugar, salt and soy sauce into a small flameproof pan or potjie, then stir well and bring to a simmer over some coals or a few flames. Naturally, this can also be done on a stove.
4. Simmer for about 6 minutes, until the sugar has dissolved completely; the exact time will obviously depend on your coals or flames.
5. Mix the half tot of cornflour with a half tot of water in a suitable cup, glass or mug. Add the cornflour mixture to the sauce and stir until the sauce gets thicker. This will take about 1 minute.
6. The sauce is now ready. Remove from the fire, let it cool slightly while you braai the meat and then serve.
7. Braai the patties in a grid over very hot coals. Aim for 8 minutes' braai time in total, only turning once.
8. Bacon must be cooked crispy. The easiest and tastiest way to achieve this is on a braai grid over the coals. Lay the pieces out carefully, so that they don't fall through the grid, and only turn them once on the braai. If there's space on your grid, do this at the same time that you're braaing the patties. Remove from the fire when ready.
9. Also braai the pineapple slices for 5 minutes on each side so that they caramelise and sweeten.
10. Butter or oil the sliced rolls and toast on the grid, taking care not to over-toast (burn) them.
11. Assemble the burger: Roll, lettuce, tomato, patty, mozzarella cheese, pineapple, bacon, sweet-chilli sauce.

THE BASH BURGER

This method of braaing a burger patty is the route to extra-crispy outsides yet a juicy centre. Here you do not pre-make or form the patties before going to the fire but simply divide the mince into portions. When everything else is ready, you put those portions of mince on a searing-hot cast-iron plate or pan and then use a flat object to – in one swift movement between the plate and chosen object – bash (smash, strike, hit, beat, thump, slap, smack, batter, pound, pummel, thrash, rap, buffet, hammer, bang, knock, wallop, belt, whack, clout, clip, clobber, bop, biff, sock, deck) each portion of meat into a flatter form, resembling a patty, which will be uniformly flat but not perfectly round.

Some basic guidelines:
- You need something to bash the burgers with. A heavy spatula made from metal will do the job. A truffle designed to plaster walls with cement also works very well, but definitely use one that hasn't actually been used to plaster walls with cement.
- Use a cast-iron grill pan that you can place directly on the fire. You need a flat surface that can handle very high heat. If you don't own this device, use the upside-down lid of your potjie.
- The less you handle or touch the meat, the better. You want loose ground beef. The more you mould it, the more packed it will become and that is not what you want to achieve as you want lots of air pockets in the beef mince so that the juices and fat released during the cooking can sit there and end up in your mouth. If you press out all the air pockets, the juices have nowhere to accumulate in the patty and will drift away.
- Bashing the meat means that some pieces of mince get very acquainted with the cast iron, and those pieces get very crispy.
- All you need to add to the beef mince is salt and pepper – nothing else. This can be done during the braai.

WHAT YOU NEED
(makes 4)

FOR THE BURGER
500 g lean beef mince
4 hamburger rolls
olive oil
salt and pepper
120 g good-quality Cheddar cheese (sliced or grated)

FOR THE SAUCE
½ cup mayonnaise (creamy)
1 tot tomato sauce
1 tot Dijon mustard
1 gherkin (normal-sized, chopped)
1 tsp garlic powder
1 tsp paprika
½ tsp cayenne pepper

WHAT TO DO

1. Prepare your sauce first: Add all the ingredients together and use your stick blender or food processor to convert into a smooth sauce. Failing these gadgets, your last resort will just be to chop the gherkin really fine and just mix it all together.
2. Divide your mince into four heaps. Do not handle the meat too much. Using your recently washed hands, form the meat into a ball very lightly and remember to keep the edges of the meat edgy and loose.
3. Position your cast-iron pan directly over the flames to get a searing-hot surface. Pour a little bit of oil on the pan.
4. Place the four balls of meat on the hot surface and swiftly apply a single moment of pressure onto each of them with your chosen weapon, ensuring they are uniformly flat and roughly the size of patties. Season with salt and pepper.
5. After a minute or two, when you can see the meat colour changing as it cooks, flip the patties over using your spatula to scrape it loose from the grill pan. Season the other side with salt and pepper. Immediately also add cheese to each patty. Braai the other side for another 2 or 3 minutes.
6. During this process, oil the sliced rolls and toast on the grill pan, taking care not to over-toast (burn) them.
7. Assemble the burger: Roll, patty straight off the fire, sauce, roll.

IRISH WILD WEST COAST BURGER

This recipe was born during a tour along the Irish West Coast, known as the Wild Atlantic Way. The inspiration comes from their most-prized local product, Guinness stout beer. Anyone lucky enough to have visited Ireland and eaten many a steak-and-Guinness pie in many a pub, knows how well this type of beer combines with beef. To this, I added two other excellent ingredients available throughout Ireland: Irish cheese and high-quality smoked bacon.

Although I generally steer away from pre-made burger patties, this recipe calls for them. Homemade patties might disintegrate during the marinating and braaing process, and the beer will marinate and dominate the taste of the meat so much anyway that you might as well take the easy store-bought patty route here. So if your local butcher has been trying to get you to test his burger patties for years, now is your chance! Most supermarkets sell packs of fresh burger patties which are also fine for this recipe. Where available, go for the larger or oversized ones.

WHAT YOU NEED
(makes 4)

4 high-quality hamburger patties
4 hamburger rolls
1 dark stout beer
120 g aged white Cheddar cheese (sliced or grated)
1 packet bacon
butter or olive oil

WHAT TO DO

1. Place the burger patties in a marinade bowl and pour the beer over them so that they are all comfortably covered in beer. If the patties are covered in beer and you still have beer left in the can or bottle, drink the rest of the beer. Cover the bowl, put it in a fridge and let them marinate for a few hours or preferably overnight.
2. Braai the patties over high heat for about 8 minutes until done. You only need to turn the patties once during the braai. During the final 2 minutes of the braai, place cheese on top of each patty so that the heat of the meat and the heat of the fire can melt the cheese.
3. At the same time that you are braaing the patties, also braai the bacon – you can do this quite easily and successfully on a normal grid over the coals of a fire.
4. Butter or oil the sliced rolls and toast on the grid, taking care not to over-toast (burn) them.
5. Assemble the burger: Buttered and toasted roll, patty topped with melted cheese, braaied bacon, roll.

AND ...

It's not absolutely necessary to use a particular brand of dark stout beer for this recipe. Use the one you have or can find.

ROGAN JOSH BURGER

When I make potjie, it's not always a half-day job. I do believe that you can also focus your efforts on making life as much fun and hassle-free as possible. And so my original Rogan Josh Curry Potjie recipe does not involve knuckles, necks or any other tough cut of stewing meat but rather, deboned bite-sized chunks of lamb meat, which amongst other things, means you go from lighting the fire to serving the feast in 1 hour. Simply speaking, I don't have a day to wait every time the Rogan Josh craving speaks to me. Naturally, this evolved into sometimes making said feast not with a wonderful bit of leg of lamb meat, but by simply cutting beef steaks down to size and having a wonderfully fragrant Beef Rogan Josh Potjie ready in well under an hour. As you might imagine, this is often served with roti or roosterkoek – which led me to this burger. Same basic ingredients, quicker to make, same tried-and-tested winning flavour profile and neatly packaged as a burger. A natural evolution paying proud homage to its origin in beauty, texture and taste.

WHAT YOU NEED
(makes 4)

FOR THE BURGER
500 g lean beef mince (or 4 hamburger patties)
4 hamburger rolls
butter or olive oil
cucumber (12 slices)
2 tomatoes (sliced)
1 punnet fresh coriander

FOR THE SAUCE
2 tots olive oil
1 onion (peeled and finely chopped)
4 garlic cloves (crushed or chopped)
fresh ginger (crushed or chopped, equal in volume to the garlic)
1 bay leaf
1 tot paprika
1 tsp cinnamon
1 tsp ground coriander
1 tsp ground cumin
1 tsp salt
½ tsp pepper
½ tsp cayenne pepper
½ tsp cloves (powder)
½ cup water
1 cup plain yoghurt

WHAT TO DO

1. Convert the 500 g lean beef mince into four equally sized, 100% pure-beef patties. Pure mince binds perfectly for a great patty – don't add anything like onion, breadcrumbs, egg, spices, salt or pepper. Your two recently washed hands are entirely capable of forming patties from mince but a patty press makes the job even easier.

2. Make the sauce: Heat the oil in your fireproof pan or pot and sauté the onion until soft. Add the garlic and ginger and fry for about 1 minute and then add all of the other spices. Right about now, you will smell some great things happening in the pot as the heat starts to release fragrances from the spices. Continue to fry the spices until things start to get overly sticky at the bottom of the potjie. Now add the water and use the water to scrape loose any bits that might be stuck on the bottom of the potjie. Let the sauce simmer until most of the water has cooked off and then add the yoghurt while stirring continuously to properly combine it with everything else. Let the sauce continue to simmer gently, stirring often enough that it doesn't burn, continuing to reduce it slightly while you braai the patties.

3. Braai the patties in a grid over very hot coals. Aim for 8 minutes' braai time in total, only turning once. To avoid the patties getting stuck to the grid, you can use a combination of the following tactics: Use a grid with thicker rods; spray the grid with non-stick spray; gently lay the patties onto the grid so that you're not squeezing them into the grid; braai over very hot coals so that the patties seal before sinking into the grid; move the patties slightly with your braai tongs or spatula just as they start to braai and seal, so that ever-so-slightly braaied meat (as opposed to completely raw meat) touches the grid. As the meat cooks, it naturally starts loosening from the grid. Now, only turn the patties once and do that gently.

4. Butter or oil the insides of the cut rolls and toast on the grid, taking care not to over-toast (burn) them.

5. Assemble the burger: Roll, cucumber, tomato, patty, Rogan Josh sauce, fresh coriander, roll.

THE GARLIC BURGER

With this burger we are not going to beat about the garlic plantation. It is our explicit intention to have the recognisable flavour of garlic ever present. Let's clear something up – there is no such thing as 'breath that stinks of garlic'. What these counter-garlic revolutionaries are actually trying to say is, 'You carry the pleasant smell of garlic; I am jealous of the great meal you had.' Garlic is very healthy for you and has been used by humans to flavour food for over 7 000 years. If you have friends who make you feel uncomfortable about your abundant culinary use of garlic, my suggestion is that you simply cut them from your circle of trust. Alternatively, give them a fair warning not to attend your garlic burger braai!

WHAT YOU NEED
(makes 4)

500 g lean beef mince (or 4 high-quality hamburger patties)

4 hamburger rolls

1 roll/slab garlic and herb butter

potentially more butter

6 garlic cloves (crushed and finely chopped – this is enough if the cloves are a decent size; otherwise use more because you want the sauce to have a strong taste of garlic)

1 tot white bread or cake flour

1 cup milk

1 cup cream

1 cup aged white Cheddar cheese (grated)

lettuce

2 tomatoes (sliced)

salt and freshly ground pepper

WHAT TO DO

1. Make the patties: Cut four disks of about 1 cm thick from the roll or slab of garlic butter. Use your wet hands, recently washed with soap and then rinsed with cold water, to divide the mince into 4 evenly sized balls and then form the patties around the disks of butter. The idea is to have firm patties with the butter disks at the centre. In practice, you put a disk of butter on a ball of mince, push it right to the middle of the mince with one of your thumbs and then form the patty around it. To flatten and neaten them, I like to put them on a flat surface, press down on the patty with the palm of one hand and pat them all around the side with the other hand. Put the patties on a plate and refrigerate until you're ready to braai them.
2. Make the creamy garlic sauce: Melt 1 tot of butter in a pot and add the garlic. Let the garlic fry for about 30 seconds and then add the tot of flour and mix well. Add a little bit of milk at a time and stir continuously. Keep on adding the milk and once it is all in, gradually add the cream and stir until all of that is in as well. Now let the mixture simmer for a few minutes. Add the cheese, stir that in and season to taste. You could theoretically perform this step while you braai the patties but I like to do it beforehand and then reheat and wake up the sauce just as it's about to be served.
3. Braai the patties: The biggest challenge is keeping the patties in one piece by ensuring that they don't stick to the grid. Put the patties down very gently. Do not press on them; do not handle them any more than is necessary, and when you turn them, do it with extreme care. Start on very high heat to seal them quickly, hopefully before they have the chance to 'sink' into the grid and get stuck. Braai the patties for about 8 minutes in total. Once on each side will do the trick so you will need to turn them only once. Don't fiddle with the patties to check whether they are sticking. As the meat starts to cook, it releases fat and juices and usually loosens itself from the grid.
4. Butter the sliced rolls and toast on the grid, taking care not to over-toast (burn) them. Depending on the size of the roll of garlic butter you set out with – and after inserting a disk of that into each patty and using some for the garlic sauce – you might now be without garlic butter. In that case, for this step, just use normal butter, which you really should always have available in your fridge.
5. Assemble the burger: Roll, lettuce, tomato, garlic-stuffed patty, creamy garlic-and-cheese sauce, roll.

CHAKALAKA BURGER

Chakalaka is the original South African spicy relish. It goes well with braaied meat and equally well with fresh bread. Make your own and naturally this comes together very well on a burger. Round it off with sour cream and take a bow.

WHAT YOU NEED
(makes 4)

500 g lean beef mince (or 4 high-quality hamburger patties)
4 hamburger rolls
olive oil
1 onion (chopped)
1 bell pepper (green, yellow or red, seeded and chopped)
1 carrot (peeled and grated, or chopped)
2 garlic cloves (crushed and chopped)
ginger (chopped or grated, equal in volume to the garlic)
2 tsp medium curry powder
1 tin or sachet tomato paste (around 50 g)
½ cup liquid (water, wine, beer, cider or juice)
salt and pepper
sour cream (a 250 ml tub is more than enough)

WHAT TO DO

1. Convert the 500 g lean beef mince into four equally sized, 100% pure-beef patties. Pure mince binds perfectly for a great patty – don't add anything like onion, breadcrumbs, egg, spices, salt or pepper. Your two recently washed hands are entirely capable of forming patties from mince but a patty press makes the job even easier.
2. Make the sauce: Heat 2 tots of oil in your fireproof pan or pot and sauté the onion, pepper and carrot until soft. Then add the garlic and ginger and fry for another minute. Add the curry powder and tomato paste and fry for a minute to release the flavours of the spices. When things become too sticky at the bottom of the pan, add a dash of water to loosen the sticky bits and scrape all along the bottom to ensure nothing burns. In principle, the chakalaka is ready but will get better with time, so add half a cup of liquid, stir that in and let it simmer while you braai the patties. During this time, add salt and pepper to taste.
3. Braai the patties in a grid over very hot coals. Aim for 8 minutes' braai time in total, only turning once. To avoid the patties getting stuck to the grid, you can use a combination of the following tactics: Use a grid with thicker rods; spray the grid with non-stick spray; gently lay the patties onto the grid so that you're not squeezing them into the grid; braai over very hot coals so that the patties seal before sinking into the grid; move the patties slightly with your braai tongs or spatula just as they start to braai and seal, so that ever-so-slightly braaied meat (as opposed to completely raw meat) touches the grid. As the meat cooks, it naturally starts loosening from the grid. Now, only turn the patties once and do that gently.
4. Oil the insides of the cut rolls and toast on the grid, taking care not to over-toast (burn) them.
5. Assemble the burger: Roll, patty, chakalaka, sour cream, roll.

BURGUNDY BURGER

The Burgundy region of France is notable for a few things. The town of Dijon gave the world Dijon mustard and then there is their obsession with Burgundy wines – the Burgundies – namely Chardonnay and pinot noir. In an ideal world, you would top the Burgundy burger with one of the famous soft Burgundy cheeses, but to my mind, they are prohibitively expensive in South Africa. As such, I'm giving you the choice of easily available Brie or Camembert – both French in origin and from neighbouring provinces of Burgundy.

WHAT YOU NEED
(makes 4)

500 g lean beef mince (or 4 high-quality hamburger patties)
4 hamburger rolls
butter or olive oil
3 onions (sliced)
2 garlic cloves (crushed)
2 tots Chardonnay (or any other white wine)
2 tots Dijon mustard
½ cup mayonnaise (creamy)
1 whole round (about 125 g) **Camembert or Brie cheese** (sliced)
1 punnet fresh rocket leaves

WHAT TO DO

1. Convert the 500 g lean beef mince into four equally sized, 100% pure-beef patties. Pure mince binds perfectly for a great patty – don't add anything like onion, breadcrumbs, egg, spices, salt or pepper. Your two recently washed hands are entirely capable of forming patties from mince but a patty press makes the job even easier.
2. Heat some butter or oil in a pan and fry the onion and garlic until soft. Add the white wine and simmer for 20 minutes or more until most of the liquid is gone and the onions look nicely caramelised.
3. Braai the patties in a grid over very hot coals. Aim for 8 minutes' braai time in total, only turning once. To avoid the patties getting stuck to the grid, you can use a combination of the following tactics: Use a grid with thicker rods; spray the grid with non-stick spray; gently lay the patties onto the grid so that you're not squeezing them into the grid; braai over very hot coals so that the patties seal before sinking into the grid; move the patties slightly with your braai tongs or spatula just as they start to braai and seal, so that ever-so-slightly braaied meat (as opposed to completely raw meat) touches the grid. As the meat cooks, it naturally starts loosening from the grid. Now, only turn the patties once and do that gently.
4. During the braai, you can mix the mustard and mayonnaise, and cut the cheese into slices. Rocket leaves generally don't need much attention by way of preparation.
5. Butter or oil the sliced rolls and toast on the grid, taking care not to over-toast (burn) them.
6. Assemble the burger: Roll, mayonnaise and mustard mix, rocket leaves, patty, cheese, onions, roll.

SPICED BACON AND CHEESE BURGER

For a stage of my life, all burgers I made were bacon and cheese burgers and on page 120 of this book you can find my original bacon and cheese burger recipe, made with braaied homemade pure-beef patties, braaied bacon and a cheese sauce. This recipe comes from a recipe crowdsourcing project I embarked on a few years ago and here we don't assemble the sum of the whole after braaing the individual parts but actually put the bacon and cheese right into the patty, which is a great new take on an old classic. While you're at it, you might add a few other things as well.

WHAT YOU NEED
(makes 4)

500 g lean beef mince
4 hamburger rolls
1 packet bacon (diced)
120 g Cheddar cheese (grated)
1 medium-sized onion (grated)
2 tsp paprika
1 tsp dried mixed herbs
1 tsp ground cumin
1 tsp ground pepper
butter or olive oil
lettuce
2 tomatoes (sliced)
2 gherkins (sliced)
2 tots mayonnaise (creamy)

WHAT TO DO

1. Fry the bacon in a pan on your fire or on a stove. Let it cool down.
2. Now add all of the ingredients for the patties to a bowl. That means the fried bacon bits, beef mince, Cheddar cheese, grated onion, paprika, herbs, cumin and pepper. Thoroughly mix everything together, aiming for an even distribution.
3. Convert the spiced minced mixture into four equally sized patties. These patties will be slightly more fragile than the 100% pure-beef mince patties we make in most other recipes in this book but will still bind perfectly fine without the need for impurities like breadcrumbs or eggs. Your two recently washed hands are entirely capable of forming patties from mince but a patty press makes the job even easier.
4. Braai the patties in a grid over very hot coals. Aim for 8–10 minutes' braai time in total, only turning once. To avoid the patties getting stuck to the grid, you can use a combination of the following tactics: Use a grid with thicker rods; spray the grid with non-stick spray; gently lay the patties onto the grid so that you're not squeezing them into the grid; braai over very hot coals so that the patties seal before sinking into the grid; move the patties slightly with your braai tongs or spatula just as they start to braai and seal, so that ever-so-slightly braaied meat (as opposed to completely raw meat) touches the grid. As the meat cooks, it naturally starts loosening from the grid. Now, only turn the patties once and do that gently.
5. Butter or oil the sliced rolls and toast on the grid, taking care not to over-toast (burn) them.
6. Assemble the burger: Roll, lettuce, tomato, patty, gherkins, mayonnaise, roll.

SLOPPY JAN

A Sloppy Jan is essentially like a sloppy joe, but made on the braai fire. You start with a basic spicy Bolognese sauce, served on a roll and finished with grated cheese. The original recipe was sent to me on the Jan Braai Facebook page a few years ago. Try as I might, I could not find the name of the person who sent it to me so if it was you, thank you from both myself and the rest of the South African braai public.

This recipe is absolutely perfect for entertaining a large crowd with minimum effort; for example, when watching a game of sport on the television, as you can do all the hard work before the kickoff. It has a wide margin of error in terms of when it needs to be served, so you can have the potjie gently simmering away and whenever somebody is hungry, they can simply dish up for themselves. Thus, it's also a winner for easy entertainment at your house party. Naturally, you can simply double or triple the recipe to serve more people.

WHAT YOU NEED
(makes 8)

1 kg lean beef mince
8 soft hamburger rolls
butter or olive oil
1 onion (chopped)
2 garlic cloves (crushed and chopped)
1 green bell pepper (seeded and chopped)
1 tsp salt
½ tsp black pepper
less than 1 tsp cayenne pepper (optional)
1 tsp mustard powder
1 tot sugar (white or brown)
1 tot paprika
1 tot Worcestershire sauce
1 tin or sachet tomato paste (around 50 g)
1 tin chopped tomatoes
1 cup beef stock
240 g Cheddar cheese (grated, optional)
1 cup sour cream (optional)

WHAT TO DO

1. Heat a tot of butter or oil in your potjie on the fire and fry the onion until soft and cooked. Add the garlic and green pepper and continue to fry until both look like you think they should look.
2. Add the beef mince, salt and pepper and fry until the mince is cooked and brown. During this time, use your wooden spoon to break up any lumps of meat.
3. Now add the cayenne pepper, mustard powder, sugar, paprika, Worcestershire sauce and tomato paste. Now toss everything to let the spices gather some attitude for a minute or two.
4. Next you add the tin of chopped tomatoes and the cup of beef stock. Mix everything well, put the lid on the potjie and let it simmer for 30 minutes.
5. After 30 minutes, remove the lid and continue to let it simmer for another 30 minutes, uncovered. After a total cooking time of 1 hour, the meal can be served as soon as the sauce has reduced enough and you are happy with its consistency. It can also gently simmer for hours – it will just get better. Just check on the potjie now and again and if it runs dry and wants to burn, add a bit of water, wine or beer and stir it in.
6. Butter or oil the sliced rolls and toast on the grid, taking care not to over-toast (burn) them.
7. Build it: Roll, beef mince, cheese or sour cream, roll.

AND ...

A note on the cayenne pepper: it can be replaced with chilli powder. Whether you use cayenne pepper or normal chilli powder, 5 ml is on the upper edge for this recipe and sensitive palates. If no one is fussy, add a whole teaspoon, but aim for about half a teaspoon if some guests don't like a bit of burn. Technically, what you need is 'a pinch of cayenne pepper' but 'a pinch' is not a measuring unit so I refuse to put that in the ingredients list of a recipe in my book. If you don't like spicy food or want to serve this meal to children, simply leave out the cayenne pepper or chilli powder altogether.

LAMB BURGER

WHAT YOU NEED
(makes 4)

FOR THE BURGER

500 g lamb mince
4 hamburger rolls
butter or olive oil
1 tsp coriander seeds
1 tsp cumin seeds
1 tsp salt
1 tsp black pepper
2 garlic cloves
1 smallish onion (or half a big one, finely chopped)
1 tot fresh mint
1 tot fresh parsley
1 tot fresh oregano
4 rosemary twigs (optional)

FOR THE TZATZIKI

1 cup Greek yoghurt
½ cucumber (chopped)
1 tot olive oil
2 garlic cloves (crushed and chopped; more if, like me, you like garlic)
1 tot fresh parsley and mint mix (chopped)
salt and pepper
1 lemon (a few squeezes)

FOR THE SALAD

2 tomatoes (or 12 cherry tomatoes, chopped)
½ cucumber (the other half)
1 tub (200 g) **feta cheese**
olive oil

Lamb mince is usually made from the neck, breast, thick rib, flank, or trimmings of the more popular braai cuts. Unfortunately, it's quite hard to get hold of and not always available at butcheries. Lamb burgers are thus an opportunistic meal. Ask the butcher whether he has lamb mince on hand and if he does, cancel your other plans.

WHAT TO DO

1. Use a pestle and mortar and crush the coriander, cumin, salt, pepper and garlic. Finely chop the onion, mint, parsley and oregano. Mix this with the lamb mince and all the crushed spices.
2. Convert the spiced lamb mince into four equally sized patties. Your two recently washed hands are entirely capable of forming patties from mince but a patty press makes the job even easier.
3. Make the tzatziki sauce first by combining all its ingredients – and only adding salt, pepper and a few squeezes of lemon juice to taste.
4. Make the salad by chopping and combining the tomatoes, cucumber and feta cheese. Add a bit of olive oil to give it that nice shine.
5. Braai the patties in a grid over very hot coals. Aim for 10 minutes' braai time in total, only turning once. To avoid the patties getting stuck to the grid, you can use a combination of the following tactics: Use a grid with thicker rods; spray the grid with non-stick spray; gently lay the patties onto the grid so that you're not squeezing them into the grid; braai over very hot coals so that the patties seal before sinking into the grid; move the patties slightly with your braai tongs or spatula just as they start to braai and seal, so that ever-so-slightly braaied meat (as opposed to completely raw meat) touches the grid. As the meat cooks, it naturally starts loosening from the grid. Now, only turn the patties once and do that gently.
6. Butter or oil the insides of the cut rolls and toast on the grid, taking care not to over-toast (burn) them.
7. Assemble the burger: Roll, patty, tzatziki sauce, salad, roll.
8. Because it looks cool, you have the option of keeping it all together by inserting a rosemary sprig (with all its leaves removed, except for the top few) through the middle of the burger from top to bottom. Failing that, you can also use a sosatie stick.

AND …

If you can't find fresh mint, parsley or oregano, then leave out what you don't have and make a note to upgrade your herb garden next weekend. These are basic herbs that grow easily in most parts of South Africa. You really should have them. Original tzatziki recipes tell you to first salt the cucumber to dry it out and make the sauce firmer. You don't really have to do it but now you know, just in case you ever end up discussing tzatziki sauce with a distant Greek relative of the bride at a friend's wedding.

PORK NECK BURGER

Pork neck steaks are a great choice for the braai as they are generally quite tender and have fantastic marbling, with the small bits of fat keeping the meat juicy during the braai while at the same time, imparting flavour to the meat. Pork should be braaied more well (to the done side of medium) than beef or lamb, and that means there is an increased risk the meat will be dry by the time it is ready to eat. In this recipe, we manage that potential problem by adding cheese on top of each steak during the final stages of the braai. The cheese will melt, add great taste and texture, and counteract any danger of a dry piece of meat. We know mustard and cheese go well together and we know mustard and pork are good braai mates. Together, the three of them give you a burger that tastes great and can easily be prepared on the road as you need so few ingredients and little equipment for it!

Your first choice for meat here is pork neck steaks and not pork neck chops, as the latter have a piece of bone in them. If you can't find pork neck steaks, go for deboned pork loin chops/steaks. Failing that, debone some yourself by simply cutting the bones out of the steaks.

WHAT YOU NEED
(makes 4)

4 pork neck steaks
4 hamburger rolls
Dijon and/or wholegrain mustard
salt
120 g Cheddar cheese
(sliced or grated)
butter or olive oil

WHAT TO DO

1. 'Butter' each pork neck steak on both sides with mustard. Technically, we could also say 'mustard' each pork neck steak on both sides. Use Dijon, wholegrain or a combination of the two.
2. Braai the meat over hot coals for about 10–15 minutes until done. You want to turn them fairly regularly so that the mustard on the steaks doesn't burn. During this time, you can also sprinkle or grind a bit of salt onto each piece of meat.
3. During the final minute or two of the braai, place the cheese onto each piece of meat. The heat of the meat and fire should melt the cheese.
4. Butter or oil the sliced rolls and toast on the grid, taking care not to over-toast (burn) them.
5. Insert each braaied pork neck steak into a roll and enjoy!

AND …

For me this recipe ticks all the boxes of greatness: easy ingredients, minimal preparation, easy to do, looks good and tastes great. If you're on a road trip and the craving to braai speaks to you, answer its call with this one.

PORK BELLY BURGER

I always give credit where it's due – in this case, a street market in the Japanese city of Kobe, a city where you would think a man should spend all his time eating steak, especially if that man is a visiting tourist from South Africa with a particular interest in things like steak. I did have some steaks during my visit but the pork belly roll I had from a street vendor on my first night's walk-through of the city was so incredibly good that I spent the following night circling that stand, eating a few pork belly rolls and committing to memory exactly what needed to be done and improved back home to get to where we are here – the greatest braaied pork belly burger in the world.

WHAT YOU NEED
(makes 4)

FOR THE BURGER
4 hamburger rolls
butter or olive oil
1 baby cabbage (shredded)
2 carrots (grated)
½ cup mayonnaise (creamy)

FOR THE PORK BELLY
1 kg pork belly (ask your butcher for one with a relatively thin layer of fat)
1 cup soy sauce
1 cup chicken stock
1 cup orange juice
peeled rind of 1 orange (solid peel, not grated or zested)
1 whole star anise
1 cinnamon stick
1 tot fresh ginger (crushed or chopped)
½ cup brown sugar

WHAT TO DO

1. Score the fat of the pork belly. This means you must use a sharp knife to cut a criss-cross pattern into the outer layer of fat.
2. Throw all the ingredients for the meat into your potjie and stir. Now add the pork belly fat side up and spoon some of the marinade over the top.
3. Close the potjie with the lid and let the potjie simmer on low heat for 2 hours. You want a gentle simmer. Once or twice during the cooking process, you can open the lid of the potjie to spoon more of the sauce onto the meat.
4. At some stage during the 2 hours of simmering, mix the cabbage, carrot and mayonnaise, and set aside in your fridge for later.
5. After 2 hours or more (once the meat is completely cooked and visibly soft and tender when you prod it with tongs or a fork), remove the pork from the potjie. Put the meat on a wooden cutting board and let it rest for a few minutes. Leave the potjie on the fire so that the sauce left in there can reduce.
6. Slice the meat into four equally sized slices and pack these flat into your hinged grid. Now braai these very tender belly pieces over hot coals until crispy on both sides.
7. Butter or oil the insides of the cut rolls and toast on the grid, taking care not to over-toast (burn) them.
8. Assemble the burger: Roll, coleslaw, pork belly, additional sauce from potjie, roll.

CHORIPÁN BURGER

Being entirely subjective, I can factually say that South Africans are the best braaiers in the world. If you really want to see how to cook food on a fire, come to South Africa. And by South Africa, I also mean our adopted fellow southern Africans in neighbouring countries like Namibia, Botswana, Zimbabwe and Mozambique.

But there are a few other nations around the world that also know their way around the braai fire. In Argentina I was fortunate enough to have experienced a few quite extensive braais – or as they call it, asado. What boerewors is to a South African braai, chorizo is to Argentina. Not the cured and dried sausage from Spain – no, in Argentina the chorizo is a fresh sausage; the spicy cousin of boerewors, you braai it like you would braai boerewors. It's a staple item at any asado and you serve it as is, or on a roll, in which case you would call it a choripán. And what chutney is to a boerewors roll, chimichurri sauce is to a choripán.

Subsequent to experiencing this culinary delight in Argentina I set about creating a South African version. But as this style of chorizo is not widely available in South Africa, you start off by using the mince of pork boerewors and giving that the flavour profile of chorizo. Instead of making the effort of stuffing that back into casings, just braai chorizo patties and serve it in the shape of a burger.

WHAT YOU NEED
(makes 4)

FOR THE BURGER
500–600 g high-quality pork boerewors (I obviously suggest Jan Braai Varkwors)
4 hamburger rolls
1 tot white vinegar
1 tot paprika
1 tsp chilli powder
1 tsp garlic powder
1 tsp cumin powder
1 tsp dried oregano
1 tsp dried marjoram
butter or olive oil

FOR THE SAUCE
4 long red chillies (deseeded and chopped)
4 long green chillies (deseeded and chopped)
2 garlic cloves (crushed and chopped)
½ tot dried oregano
1 tsp coarse salt
1 tsp ground black pepper
1 tot white wine vinegar
2 tots olive oil
½ cup flat leaf parsley

WHAT TO DO

1. Prepare the sauce: Grab your stick blender or food processor (or if there's loadshedding, your pestle and mortar) and convert all of the ingredients for the sauce into exactly that – a sauce.

2. Make the patties. In a mixing bowl, combine the vinegar and all the herbs and spices. Now remove the pork mince from the boerewors casing. The easiest way to do this is to use a sharp knife and slice open the casing whilst it's still in the punnet. Then, scrape out all the mince into the bowl and thoroughly mix this with the spice slurry. Use your patty press or recently washed hands to convert the spiced mince into four equally sized patties.

3. Braai the patties in a grid over fairly hot coals. Aim for around 10 minutes' braai time in total, either only turning once if the patties are fragile, or three times if you think they are looking solid. The spices in this patty increase the chance that you'll burn the patties so we are taking an ever-so-slightly-less-aggressive braai approach than we would for regulation, pure-beef mince patties. To avoid the patties getting stuck to the grid, you can use a combination of the following tactics: Use a grid with thicker rods; spray the grid with non-stick spray; gently lay the patties onto the grid so that you're not squeezing them into the grid; move the patties slightly with your braai tongs or spatula just as they start to braai and seal, so that ever-so-slightly braaied meat (as opposed to completely raw meat) touches the grid. As the meat cooks, it naturally starts loosening from the grid. Now, only turn the patties once and do that gently.

4. Butter or oil the insides of the cut rolls and toast on the grid, taking care not to over-toast (burn) them.

5. Assemble the burger: Roll, patty, sauce, roll.

PULLED PORK PARTY

WHAT YOU NEED
(makes 10)

FOR THE PORK

2 kg deboned pork shoulder
(or other piece of pork meat)

1 tsp pepper

1 tsp cumin

1 tsp mustard powder

1 tsp cayenne pepper

1 tsp salt

1 tot paprika

1 tot brown sugar

FOR THE POTJIE

1 tot olive oil

1 onion (sliced)

4 garlic cloves (crushed)

2 cups chicken stock

1 cup additional liquid
(beer, cider, juice or ginger ale)

FOR THE RANCH SAUCE

1 bottle (500 ml) **buttermilk** (2 cups)

1 tub (250 ml) **sour cream** (1 cup)

3 tots chives (freshly chopped)

1 tot Dijon mustard

1 lemon (juice and zest)

1 tsp garlic powder

1 tsp salt

1 tsp pepper

The concept of pulled pork is very simple. We start with quite a cheap cut of meat that is fairly tough. The meat is generously spiced until it has a real attitude and we then slow-cook it in a potjie until it's so soft we can just pull it apart. Pulled pork is not really a meal for two. The size of the meat and the time it takes to prepare means that when it's pulled pork, it's a party!

This recipe is incredibly easy, especially if you follow it. Phone you butcher ahead of time and ask him to prepare a 2 kg piece of deboned pork shoulder. For a competent butcher, this is a piece of cake and it's not a particularly expensive cut of meat either. Failing this, 2 kg of pork shoulder on the bone will work just as well. Supermarkets generally sell pieces of pork meat of roughly this size. Your weapon of choice here is a no. 2 or no. 3 three-legged potjie or a no. 10 flat-bottomed one. You make the dressing sauce ahead of time and you'll also do most of the work for the pork a few hours in advance. By the time your party guests arrive, all you need to do is occasionally add a few coals under the potjie and of course, serve up a great meal.

WHAT TO DO

1. To make the sauce, you shake the bottle of buttermilk before opening its top. Now throw that and all the other ingredients for the sauce in a bowl or jug and mix well. Cover whatever the sauce is in and put it in your fridge until you're ready to serve the meal.
2. Prepare the meat by mixing all the spices together, then rub the spice blend into the pork shoulder.
3. Get some flames under the potjie, add the oil and onion, and fry the onion for a few minutes.
4. Now add the garlic and the whole chunk of pork to the potjie.
5. Brown the pork shoulder on all sides. You can take as long as you like to do this but aim for 10 minutes.
6. Your cooking liquid should be 3 cups in total – 2 cups of stock and 1 cup of additional liquid. Add all 3 cups to the potjie and let the potjie heat up to a gentle simmer. Now close the lid. The potjie should bubble very slowly for 3–4 hours until the meat is very soft and starts to fall apart by itself. Every half hour or so, you can lift the lid and flip the meat over. If at any time the potjie is running dry, add a bit more cooking liquid, using any of the options.
7. When the pork is done, remove from the fire and let it rest somewhere to relax a bit. Use two forks to pull apart and shred the pork. Taste a piece and congratulate yourself. Now mix all the pulled pork with all the remaining liquid in the potjie.
8. Your guests can build their own creations by piling a generous helping of pulled pork meat onto a sliced roll, and topping it with ranch sauce, slices of gherkin and slices of onion.

AND ...

Make up the rolls with 10 soft hamburger rolls (sliced), 4 big gherkins (sliced into thin strips with a vegetable peeler) and 1 red onion (thinly sliced).

SHERRY BOEREWORS SLIDERS

A 'slider' is the culinary term for a miniature hamburger or more accurately, a small piece of meat served on a mini bread roll. Forming and braaing miniature little patties has always seemed like far too much hard work to me, as both the preparation and the braaing would be complex. Boerewors was an easy solution to this.

My other problem with sliders is that they are sometimes heavy on the bread and light on the meat. Again, this is something we can solve by simply not closing them with another piece of bread, thereby upping our ratio of meat to bread.

Sherry, the original Old Brown type, is a very good value-for-money product to braai with, and one of the core ingredients of this recipe. The sweetness of the sherry complements the spiciness of the boerewors perfectly.

WHAT YOU NEED
(makes about 30 pieces)

1,2 kg boerewors (I suggest Jan Braai Original Boerewors)
1 long fresh baguette
2 cups sherry
butter and olive oil
3 onions (finely chopped)
3 garlic cloves (crushed and chopped)
skewers

WHAT TO DO

1. Cut the raw boerewors into pieces of about 6 cm each.
2. Put the pieces of meat into a bowl and pour the sherry over them. Cover the bowl and let the boerewors marinate in a fridge for a few hours.
3. Remove the boerewors pieces from the sherry and skewer them. It doesn't matter how many skewers you use as it's not a case of a skewer per person. Do not discard the sherry.
4. When the fire is lit, heat up a fireproof pan or potjie and sauté the chopped onion in 1 tot of oil and 1 tot of butter for about 5 minutes. Add the garlic and sauté for another minute.
5. Pour all the sherry that the boerewors was swimming in, into the pan or potjie with the onion and garlic and bring to the boil. Stir regularly and let this cook and reduce by half.
6. Put the marinated boerewors skewers in a hinged grid, close the grid and braai over hot coals for about 8 minutes until done. Give each side at least two looks at the coals, meaning you need to turn the grid at least three times in total.
7. During the braai, you or one of your braai party members can cut the baguette in thin slices (we want maximum meat-to-bread ratio so keep the slices thin). Each slice needs a layer of butter on one side and now you may or may not want to toast them on the fire.
8. Arrange the slices of baguette on a platter and give each piece some of the sherry and onion sauce.
9. When the boerewors is ready, take it off the fire, pull out the skewers and place a piece of braaied sherry-infused boerewors on each prepared slice of baguette.

KLEIN KAROO OSTRICH BURGER

n the R62 road in the Klein Karoo lie three towns in a row, perfectly positioned for a regional dish. As you drive from Cape Town, the first one you pass through is Ladismith with its cheese factory. Next you get Calitzdorp, known for its port, and, lastly, there is Oudtshoorn, a town steeped in a rich ostrich heritage.

WHAT YOU NEED
(makes 4)

500 g ostrich mince
4 hamburger rolls
1 onion
butter
1 cup Cape Ruby port
lettuce
2 tomatoes (sliced)
120 g Cheddar cheese (grated)

WHAT TO DO

1. Convert the 500 g ostrich mince into four equally sized patties. Pure mince binds perfectly for a great patty – don't add anything like onion, breadcrumbs, egg, spices, salt or pepper. Your two recently washed hands are entirely capable of forming patties from mince but a patty press makes the job even easier.
2. Slice the onion into rings and sauté with some butter. To sauté means to fry lightly in a pan. This will take about 5 minutes.
3. Add the port and reduce until it is completely absorbed into the onions and becomes a sticky, dark-purple relish. Put to one side.
4. Braai the patties in a grid over very hot coals. Aim for 8 minutes' braai time in total, only turning once. Ostrich is not a fatty meat, so don't be scared to leave some pink in the middle of the patties. To avoid the patties getting stuck to the grid, you can use a combination of the following tactics: Use a grid with thicker rods; spray the grid with non-stick spray; gently lay the patties onto the grid so that you're not squeezing them into the grid; braai over very hot coals so that the patties seal before sinking into the grid; move the patties slightly with your braai tongs or spatula just as they start to braai and seal, so that ever-so-slightly braaied meat (as opposed to completely raw meat) touches the grid. As the meat cooks, it naturally starts loosening from the grid. Now, only turn the patties once and do that gently.
5. Butter the insides of the sliced rolls and toast on the grid, taking care not to over-toast (burn) them.
6. Assemble the burger: Roll, lettuce, tomato slices, ostrich patty, grated cheese, onion, roll.

THE REVOLUTIONARY MUSHROOM BURGER

This is a revolutionary burger. It's the vegetarian meal that meat-eaters love. I like to make these using those normal supermarket hamburger rolls with little to no substance, as it keeps the focus on the mushroom.

WHAT YOU NEED
(makes 4)

4 **giant mushrooms**
4 **soft hamburger rolls**
garlic butter
1 tub (250 g) **plain cream cheese**
feta cheese (I like the kind with bits of black pepper but any type will do)

WHAT TO DO

1. Braai the mushrooms on medium-to-hot coals until nicely browned and fairly soft, for a total of about 6–8 minutes. Braai them for 3 minutes with the bottom (black) side facing downwards. Then flip them over, scoop a bit of garlic butter into each and then braai with the top (white) side facing downwards until they are soft. They turn quite easily and if you are gentle they will not break apart, so either an open or hinged grid is fine.
2. Slice the rolls and spread cream cheese onto the bottom half of each roll.
3. Assemble the burger: Roll, cream cheese, mushroom, crumbled feta, roll.
4. The burgers can be eaten immediately and juices from the mushrooms will seep into the roll as you eat.

WHAT TO DO FOR GARLIC BUTTER

Very simply you mix chopped garlic and butter. If you have parsley on hand, you chop that and mix it in as well. For 4 mushrooms, you'll need 1–2 tots of butter, 1–2 garlic cloves and ½ tot of parsley. Alternatively, buy garlic and herb butter at a shop.

TERIYAKI TUNA BURGER

Nowadays yellowfin tuna is quite widely available around the Western Cape of South Africa. In season, thanks to a combination of commercial fishermen supplying to restaurants and shops, as well as a steady flow of tuna from fishing charters catering for both local and international tourists, you're never particularly far away from sourcing freshly caught tuna.

I am not a big fan of including recipes in my books with ingredients so prohibitively obscure or expensive that the recipe is really only there for show. My preference is recipes using ingredients that will make it possible for most readers to recreate the meals easily at home. I believe that yellowfin tuna is so easily obtainable, and also happens to be in season when the rest of the country generally heads to the Western Cape for holidays, that it warrants inclusion in a book written for everyone, to be used by all.

WHAT YOU NEED
(makes 4)

FOR THE BURGER
600 g fresh yellowfin tuna
4 hamburger rolls
sesame seeds (about 2 tots but not an exact science)
butter or olive oil
1 carrot (grated)
1 cup cabbage (thinly sliced or grated)
2 tots mayonnaise
fresh coriander

FOR THE MARINADE
½ cup dark soy sauce
½ cup sherry
2 garlic cloves (crushed and chopped)
ginger (chopped or grated, equal in volume to the garlic)
1 tot sugar

WHAT TO DO

1. Mix all the marinade ingredients together until the sugar is dissolved. Slice the tuna into four equal portions, if this is not done yet, and marinate in your fridge or cooler box for an hour or three.
2. When the fire is ready, remove the tuna from the marinade and set aside. Pour the marinade into a pot or pan and reduce by half, then remove from the fire or stove.
3. Spread sesame seeds onto a plate and put both sides of each of the marinated tuna steaks onto the sesame seeds. Now braai them over very hot coals for 2 minutes on each side and only turn once. This is also referred to as searing the tuna. It should still be a bit pink in the middle.
4. Butter or oil the insides of the cut rolls and toast on the grid, taking care not to over-toast (burn) them. You can do this at the same time as braaing the fish.
5. Mix the carrot, cabbage and mayo into the soya and sherry reduction, which by now should have cooled down a bit. A lukewarm end result for your topping is absolutely fine; in fact, ideal.
6. Assemble the burger: Roll, seared sesame-crusted teriyaki tuna steak, world-class coleslaw, fresh coriander, roll.

FISH CAKE BURGER

On a chart with ratios and graphs of the things I like to eat and actually make at home, fish cakes are an anomaly. When I see it on the blackboard of a restaurant that seems up to the task of preparing it properly, it has a good chance of being ordered. And yet as much as I like them, it's not a frequently made item at home. Plainly and simply, I think there are too many preparation steps for a dish that is brilliant yet fundamentally, is supposed to be straightforward.

As such, my advice is to never make the Fish Cake Burger from scratch. Rather read through the recipe and make a mental note to flag the opportunity when it arises. You need leftover braaied fish and you (preferably) need leftover mashed potatoes or leftover boiled potatoes to convert into mash. Once those two boxes are ticked, that's when you make fish cakes and we're good to go on a magical culinary journey.

WHAT YOU NEED
(makes 4)

FOR THE BURGER
4 hamburger rolls
butter or olive oil
fresh iceberg lettuce
2 tomatoes (sliced)
1 lemon
½ cup mayonnaise
fresh coriander or parsley

FOR THE FISH CAKES
600 g braaied or cooked fish (roughly 2 cups flaked boneless fish)
vegetable oil
2 medium-sized potatoes (cooked, cooled down and mashed)
1 bread slice (converted into crumbs in a food processor)
1 tot parsley (finely chopped)
1 egg
1 tsp salt (or less/none if your fish was seasoned during the braai)
1 tsp black pepper (or less/none if your fish was seasoned during the braai)

WHAT TO DO

1. If you are using raw fish, cook it first. The easiest way would be to braai it quickly over hot coals, or to pan-fry it in a little vegetable oil. This should not take more than 15 minutes.
2. With clean hands, flake the cooked fish (make sure you get rid of all the bones) and then combine with all the other fish cake ingredients (except the oil) in a mixing bowl. Mix well.
3. Divide the mixture into four portions and roughly manipulate into the form of patties.
4. Over a medium-hot fire, barely hotter than braaibroodjie heat, heat the oil in a large fireproof pan, paella pan or the upended lid of your cast-iron potjie. Fry the fish cakes on both sides, turning each one only once. When they are golden brown on both sides, they are ready. This should take about 8 minutes because you should be taking it easy and not burning them on the outside.
5. When they are done, consider placing the fish cakes on a couple of sheets of kitchen paper to absorb any extra oil.
6. Butter or oil the insides of the cut rolls and toast on the grid, taking care not to over-toast (burn) them.
7. Assemble the burger: Roll, lettuce, tomato, fish cake, squeeze of lemon juice, mayonnaise, fresh herbs, roll.

CAPE MALAY FISH BURGER

At home, or even on a camping trip, you will most likely serve curry with rice, or roti (if you're making a particular effort), or even both. This is not the case for a picnic braai though. Making rice out in nature is beyond the level of effort I am willing to make on an excursion that by definition should be relaxing. On a beautiful spring day a few years ago, this led to the Cape Malay Fish Burger.

Situated right next to the ocean on Cape Town's Atlantic Seaboard, between Clifton and Camps Bay, with a backdrop of the Twelve Apostles, Maiden's Cove is not only arguably, but factually, one of South Africa's most beautiful public picnic and braai areas. The soundtrack of crashing waves made me feel like fish. And as is the case with perfect spring days, there was still a nip in the air, which warranted a flavour profile with a bit of heat.

The curry sauce is pretty straightforward and you do that in your potjie or fireproof pan. Add the fish fillets and poach them until done. For this magic trick, you reduce the sauce a little beyond the point at which you would have done to serve it with rice, as the sauce needs a bit more body to hold up in your vessel of choice – a soft oversized supermarket hamburger roll. I specify hake portions in the recipe because in South African supermarkets, high-quality, frozen hake fillet packs are widely available – but obviously other suitable fresh options like yellowtail and cob will also work.

WHAT YOU NEED
(makes 4)

4 portions hake fillets (fresh or frozen)
4 hamburger rolls
butter or olive oil
1 onion (chopped)
1 bell pepper (seeded, and chopped or sliced)
1 tot curry spice (medium)
1 tin chopped tomatoes
salt and pepper
1 tub (200 g) **feta cheese**
2 tomatoes (sliced)
fresh coriander

WHAT TO DO

1. Place your potjie or fireproof pan on the fire, add the olive oil, onion and pepper, and fry until soft.
2. Add the curry spice and toss around to release the flavours. Before things get out of hand and burn, add the tin of tomatoes and mix well.
3. Add the fish fillets, season with salt and pepper and let this cook in the sauce for about 4 minutes. Gently turn the fillets around, season the other side and continue to cook until the fish is cooked and you are happy with the consistency of the sauce for burger purposes. In the unlikely event that the sauce is reduced before the fish is cooked, add a dash of water or other suitable liquid. Other suitable liquids you might have on hand include juice, wine and beer. Stock would also be suitable but it's unlikely you will have that on hand at a picnic.
4. For the final 2 minutes, as the music reaches a crescendo, crumble the feta over everything.
5. Butter or oil the insides of the cut rolls and toast on the grid, taking care not to over-toast (burn) them.
6. Assemble the burger: Roll, fresh tomato slices, fish fillet (be gentle, it might flake and break), sauce from the pan or potjie, fresh coriander, roll.

HOW TO MAKE POTATO WEDGES

It's quite evident that I braai often and that this happens on the coals of real wood fires. But I also like food prepared in other ways, and I have a few kitchen appliances to aid me in the joy of cooking food that I enjoy.

One of my favourites is my coffee machine, a classy bean-to-cup device that you fill with your choice of beans, water and milk, and at the press of a button, it makes a few noises and gives you a great cappuccino – and the wonderful smell of fresh coffee. My pasta machine needs you to fill it with flour, egg and water, and choose your shape of noodle. This revolutionary appliance then makes fresh pasta noodles in a few minutes. My ice cream machine churns and freezes the base that you prepare (which is really flavoured real custard) into the greatest ice cream south of the north pole and north of the south pole. My bread machine needs flour, yeast, water and all the normal things of bread, and diligently kneads and bakes beautiful fresh loaves without ever complaining – and makes the house smell of warm fresh bread. In the interest of full disclosure, I also have the regulation three appliances: the oven, toaster and kettle.

An appliance I never even window-shopped for though is a fryer. I find fryers antisocial and intrusive, as they literally stink. But I don't frown upon them at all and I like my friends to have them – similar to boats. I like slices of oil-fried potato, widely referred to as chips, French fries or potato wedges, as much as any normal person. I enjoy eating it at your place; I just don't want to do that in my own house. Most burgers in this book I view as a complete meal. It's enough food and a balanced meal. But sometimes you want chips. So when I do serve my burgers with chips, this is what I do.

WHAT YOU NEED
(makes 4–6)

1 kg potatoes
salted water
olive oil
coarse sea salt
1 tot paprika (optional)

WHAT TO DO

1. If relevant, rinse the potatoes of excess sand. Now parboil the potatoes in salted water until just soft, but not too soft: a fork should just be able to go in. This will take about 20 minutes. During the later stages of this 20-minute period, switch on your oven and set it to 200 °C.
2. Drain the boiled potatoes well, meaning: get all the water off. Cut into wedges, place in a large oven tray, toss around in olive oil, and generously sprinkle the wedges with coarse sea salt (and paprika if you want a bit of extra colour spice).
3. Bake in the oven at 200 °C until brown and crispy, which will take about 25 minutes. Serve with your favourite burger.

ROOSTERKOEK

Baking bread is an ancient skill, and a fulfilling one, so you need to master it. The tricky part is making the dough. If you've never made dough in your life, the recipe below will probably look quite daunting the first time you read it. Take a deep breath, drink a beer, and read it again. Like riding a bicycle, it's surprisingly easy once you get the hang of it.

WHAT YOU NEED
(makes 12 decent-sized roosterkoek)

1 kg white bread or cake flour
10 g instant yeast (it comes in 10 g packets)
1 tot sugar
½ tot salt
lukewarm water in a jug (you'll need roughly just more than 2 cups of water)
2 tots olive oil

WHAT TO DO

1. Sift the flour into a bowl that is at least three times as big as 1 kg of flour, and preferably even bigger. If you're in the middle of the bush and don't have a sieve on hand, then skip the sifting part and just chuck the flour into a big enough bowl. If you only have a 1 kg bag of flour and no more, save a little for step 10.
2. Add the yeast and sugar to the flour and mix thoroughly with your clean hands.
3. Now it's time to add the salt and toss the mixture around some more.
4. Pour in the lukewarm water bit by bit and keep kneading the dough. As soon as there is no dry flour left, you've added enough water. Take care not to add too much water, as this will lead to the dough being runny and falling through the grid. Roosterkoek falling through the grid is just no good. For 1 kg of flour, you'll probably use just a tiny bit more than 2 cups of water.
5. If you think you have enough water in there, add the 2 tots of olive oil.
6. Knead the dough well for about 10 minutes until none of it sticks to your fingers anymore and it forms one big pliable piece.
7. Cover the bowl with a kitchen towel and put in a warm area for 10 minutes.
8. Take off the kitchen towel and knead the dough again for 1 or 2 minutes.
9. Replace the kitchen towel and let it rise for at least 30 minutes.
10. Use your recently washed hands to flatten the dough onto a table or plank that is covered in flour. Also, lightly sprinkle flour on top of the dough. Your aim is to create a rectangular or square piece of dough.
11. Use a sharp knife and cut the dough into squares, and let them rise for a few minutes one final time.
12. Bake over very gentle coals for about 15–20 minutes, turning often. A roosterkoek is ready when it sounds hollow when you tap on it. Alternatively, insert the blade of your pocketknife or multi-tool into them as a test. If the blade comes out clean, the roosterkoek is ready.

AND ...

Some supermarkets sell fresh dough. If you've bought some of that, start making your roosterkoek from step 10. If you've never made dough in your life, there's no shame in asking someone who has.

CHICKEN PREGO ROLL

The thing to do with chicken breasts is make chicken burgers. You obviously need the breasts to be skinned and deboned – also known as chicken breast fillets. The typical chicken breast fillet is a bit lopsided, with a bulky part and a thin point, so put the breast fillet on a chopping board and give it a few gentle whacks on the thick part with a meat tenderising mallet before the braai. This will make it uniform in thickness, which makes for easier braaing and will soften the meat for biting through when it's on the burger. If you hit it too much, it will disintegrate, and you will be left with chicken mince. You don't want that so do be gentle with the mallet.

This is stating the obvious, but a chicken burger contains meat, salad, dairy and starch, so it really is a balanced meal all on its own.

WHAT YOU NEED
(makes 4)

FOR THE PREGO ROLLS
4 chicken breast fillets
4 hamburger rolls (preferably Portuguese rolls)
butter or olive oil
½ cup mayonnaise
lettuce
2 tomatoes (sliced)
120 g Cheddar cheese (sliced or grated)

FOR THE SAUCE
8 garlic cloves (crushed and finely chopped)
½ cup olive oil
½ cup grape vinegar (red or white)
½ cup lemon juice
½ cup water
1 tot paprika
1 tot chilli powder
1 tot salt
a few small hot chillies (piri-piri/African bird's eye, finely chopped)

WHAT TO DO

1. Finely chop the garlic and throw this into a glass bottle or jar with the oil, vinegar, lemon juice, water, paprika, chilli powder and salt. Shake well until the ingredients are mixed and all the salt dissolved.
2. Now taste the sauce and if you want it hotter, add a few finely chopped chillies to the sauce, and shake. You can add as many chillies as you wish but remember that you can never expect your guests to eat a sauce that is too hot for them. If, like me, you like quite a lot of burn, then it might be wise to mix two batches – one hot and one with fewer chillies.
3. Do not touch your eyes or any other sensitive parts of your body while you are making this sauce as the traces of chilli juice left on your hands will burn those sensitive parts. Go and wash your hands to get the chilli juices off them, and then still be careful.
4. Pack the chicken breast fillets on a chopping board and cover with cling wrap. Now pound the thick side of each piece of meat with a meat mallet, wine bottle, rolling pin, side of a meat cleaver or any other item of sufficient weight and size. You want the meat to relax so that the whole fillet is more uniform in thickness. This step will make the meat easier to braai, better-looking on your burger and more tender to bite.
5. Place the chicken in a marinating bowl and pour some of the peri-peri sauce over them. Flip them over using a tool like a spoon and get some sauce on their other sides as well. You want to coat both sides of each piece of meat, but it is not necessary for them to swim in the sauce so there will be leftover sauce, which can be used for dressing the rolls or for absolutely anything else in the following days. To be clear, the sauce used as marinade that was in touch with raw chicken needs to be discarded once it serves its purpose. You keep the rest of the sauce that you mixed for later alternative use.
6. Cover the bowl and place in a cool place like a fridge. Go and light the fire.
7. Braai the meat for about 6–10 minutes on hot coals until it is done. The nice thing about chicken breast fillets is that you can actually see the meat colour changing from raw to ready on the braai. Take the meat off the fire when ready.
8. Butter the insides of the cut rolls and toast on the grid, taking care not to over-toast (burn) them.
9. Assemble the burger: Roll, mayonnaise, lettuce, tomato, cheese, chicken breast, peri-peri sauce, roll.

CRISPY CHICKEN BURGER

On a filming trip for the *Jan Braai vir Erfenis* television show, the crew and I once went for a dhow cruise on the Zambezi River in Zimbabwe – and yes, I know that means that technically, parts of the cruise were in Zambia. The very friendly and professional company that we used provided all the liquid refreshments. These did not disappoint and included, amongst others, wine (of the type where the cork shoots out the bottle with great speed) and obviously, anti-malaria medicine in the form of gin and tonic. For some reason, we ended up having to take our own snacks though. It was described as our own 'takeaways'. Now, I cannot claim to be one who never shies away from a challenge. I actually often do exactly that. But equally often, I take a challenge head-on and revel in it. This was a case of the latter. If we were going to bring 'takeaways' on that dhow cruise in the middle of nowhere, then we would make it an iconic takeaway. And naturally, it would be done on a fire.

So before heading to Zimbabwe, we set about studying all that there is to study about crispy chicken burgers. I even got a very famous, global burger restaurant chain – the king of burgers, if you will – to take me into one of their kitchens one busy lunchtime and show me exactly how they do it. And on that dhow cruise, the crispy chicken burger was every bit as good as it should have been.

Here it is then – my well-researched, very good, crispy chicken burger, right off the fire!

WHAT YOU NEED
(makes 4)

4 chicken breast fillets
4 hamburger rolls
1 cup white bread or cake flour
1 egg (beaten)
salt and pepper
2 cups corn flake crumbs (this is a commercial product but you can also make it by abusing the version you eat for breakfast until it's a finer crumb)
butter or olive oil
iceberg lettuce (shredded)
2 tomatoes (sliced)
120 g Cheddar cheese (sliced or grated)
½ cup mayonnaise (creamy)

WHAT TO DO

1. Pack the chicken breast fillets on a chopping board and cover with cling wrap. Now pound the thick side of each piece of meat with a meat mallet, wine bottle, rolling pin, side of a meat cleaver or any other item of sufficient weight and size. You want the meat to relax so that the whole fillet is more uniform in thickness. This step will make the meat easier to braai, better-looking on your burger and more tender to bite. While the cling wrap will not aid in any of these goals, nor influence the final taste of the burger, it will prevent small pieces of chicken meat flying all over the place. If you're trying to use less plastic in your house and don't have cling wrap, don't perform this step inside the kitchen. Go and stand in the garden where small pieces of chicken meat can freely roam!
2. Find two flat bowls – one for the flour and one for the beaten egg. Season the egg with salt and pepper, then dip each chicken breast into your bowl of flour and then into the egg bowl. Be sure to cover all sides of the meat.
3. Now cover the dipped chicken breasts with the corn flake crumbs, making sure the entire breast is coated.
4. Heat some oil or butter in your fireproof pan on the fire, making sure that the pan heat is medium. You want to cook the chicken, but not burn it, so a medium temperature is important.
5. Braai the chicken fillets in the pan, turning often until they are brown and crispy all over and cooked inside.
6. Butter or oil the insides of the cut rolls and toast on the grid, taking care not to over-toast (burn) them.
7. Assemble the burger: Roll, lettuce, tomato, chicken, cheese, and mayonnaise on the top roll.

CHICKEN, CAMEMBERT, FIG AND BACON BURGER

This burger is juicy, creamy, sweet and salty. It's a dream-team combination and discovering it while braaing at home one evening was one of my inspirations for writing this book. It wasn't a flashing-light sort of moment but it did get me thinking that there's more to a braai than chops and wors. Let's emancipate the braai a bit. You can create interesting, great-tasting and beautiful-looking meals on the coals of a wood fire.

WHAT YOU NEED
(makes 4)

4 chicken breast fillets
4 hamburger rolls
olive oil
salt and black pepper
1 round (about 125 g) **Camembert cheese** (sliced)
1 packet bacon
1 packet rocket leaves (or watercress leaves)
4 ripe figs (sliced – preserved green figs are equally good)

WHAT TO DO

1. Pack the chicken breast fillets on a chopping board and cover with cling wrap. Now pound the thick side of each piece of meat with a meat mallet, wine bottle, rolling pin, side of a meat cleaver or any other item of sufficient weight and size. You want the meat to relax so that the whole fillet is more uniform in thickness. This step will make the meat easier to braai, better-looking on your burger and more tender to bite. While the cling wrap will not aid in any of these goals, nor influence the final taste of the burger, it will prevent small pieces of chicken meat flying all over the place. If you're trying to use less plastic in your house and don't have cling wrap, don't perform this step inside the kitchen. Go and stand in the garden where small pieces of chicken meat can freely roam!

2. Give each chicken fillet a light coating of olive oil. Either brush each fillet with oil or pour a bit of oil onto them and toss them around until they are all coated. Season with salt and pepper or your favourite braai salt.

3. Braai the meat for about 6–10 minutes on hot coals until it is done. The nice thing about chicken breast fillets is that you can actually see the meat colour changing from raw to ready on the braai. When you are satisfied that the chicken is almost ready and you've turned it for a final time, distribute the slices of Camembert onto the chicken breasts. You want the heat from the meat and fire to melt the cheese slightly. Now you can't turn the chicken again, as the cheese will be lost to the coals. Take the meat off the fire when ready.

4. Bacon must be cooked crispy. The easiest and tastiest way to achieve this is on a braai grid over the coals. Lay the pieces out carefully, so that they don't fall through the grid, and only turn them once on the braai. If there's space on your grid (most grids will have enough space), do this at the same time that you're braaing the chicken. Remove from the fire when ready.

5. Oil the sliced rolls and toast on the grid, taking care not to burn them.

6. Assemble the burger: Roll, rocket leaves, chicken fillet (with melted cheese), sliced figs, bacon, roll.

AND ...

You can braai the chicken, bacon and rolls at the same time, but not for the same length of time. Your aim is to have all the ingredients hot off the grid together. During the braai, your two main risks are bacon strips falling through the grid onto the coals, and bread rolls burning.

THE ROTHERHAMBURGER

The Rotherhamburger is a pretty decadent creation. It's inspired by my friend, the mythical character Seth Rotherham and his philosophy: 'Work is a sideline; live the holiday.'

WHAT YOU NEED
(makes 4)

4 chicken breast fillets
4 hamburger rolls
olive oil
salt and pepper
8 slices mozzarella cheese
8 slices bacon
8 slices salami
feta cheese (crumbled)

WHAT TO DO

1. Pack the chicken breast fillets on a chopping board and cover with cling wrap. Now pound the thick side of each piece of meat with a meat mallet, wine bottle, rolling pin, side of a meat cleaver or any other item of sufficient weight and size. You want the meat to relax so that the whole fillet is more uniform in thickness. This step will make the meat easier to braai, better-looking on your burger and more tender to bite. While the cling wrap will not aid in any of these goals, nor influence the final taste of the burger, it will prevent small pieces of chicken meat flying all over the place. If you're trying to use less plastic in your house and don't have cling wrap, don't perform this step inside the kitchen. Go and stand in the garden where small pieces of chicken meat can freely roam!
2. Give each chicken fillet a light coating of olive oil. Either brush each fillet with oil or pour a bit of oil onto them and toss them around until they are all coated. Also season the meat with salt and pepper, or your favourite braai salt.
3. Braai the meat for about 6–10 minutes on hot coals until it is done. The nice thing about chicken breast fillets is that you can actually see the meat colour changing from raw to ready on the braai. When you are satisfied that the chicken is almost ready and you've turned it for a final time, distribute the slices of mozzarella cheese onto the chicken breasts. You want the heat from the meat and fire to melt the cheese slightly. Now you can't turn the chicken again, as the cheese will be lost to the coals. Take the meat off the fire when ready.
4. Bacon must be cooked crispy. The easiest and tastiest way to achieve this is on a braai grid over the coals. Lay the pieces out carefully, so that they don't fall through the grid, and only turn them once on the braai. If there's space on your grid (most grids will have enough space), do this at the same time that you're braaing the chicken. Remove from the fire when ready.
5. Oil the insides of the cut rolls and toast on the grid, taking care not to over-toast (burn) them.
6. Assemble the burger: Roll, salami, feta, chicken (with melted mozzarella), bacon, roll.

AND …

Experiment with the salami you use for this recipe. There is a big variety out there so try things like chorizo or pepperoni to add new and interesting flavour dimensions to your burger.

THE MULE

The Mule is not so much a chicken burger as it is a braai cocktail. As all of you who have spent a decent amount of time in any great cocktail bars around the world will realise, I quite clearly based the flavour combination of the Mule on the classic cocktail by the same name. As you will see, it works very well in braaied format. Marinating the chicken breast in the ginger beer for a few hours means you end up with braaied meat that is very juicy and which sports the great complementary taste of ginger. During the braai the sugar in the marinade also creates the fantastic look, texture and taste of caramelisation on the surface of the meat. The minted mayonnaise makes the whole meal nice and fresh, something I think many a South African braai dearly needs!

WHAT YOU NEED
(makes 4)

4 chicken breast fillets
4 bread slices
1 can/bottle ginger beer
2 tots fresh mint leaves (finely chopped)
½ cup mayonnaise (creamy)
butter or olive oil
lettuce
2 tomatoes (sliced)
1 lemon

WHAT TO DO

1. Pack the chicken breast fillets on a chopping board and cover with cling wrap. Now pound the thick side of each piece of meat with a meat mallet, wine bottle, rolling pin, side of a meat cleaver or any other item of sufficient weight and size. You want the meat to relax so that the whole fillet is more uniform in thickness. This step will make the meat easier to braai, better-looking on your burger and more tender to bite. While the cling wrap will not aid in any of these goals, nor influence the final taste of the burger, it will prevent small pieces of chicken meat flying all over the place.
2. Place the chicken fillets in a marinating bowl and pour the ginger beer over them. They just need to be covered in ginger beer so depending on the shape of the bowl you might not need the whole can and there might be ginger beer left over. Drink it if there is. Let the meat marinate in a fridge for 2 hours.
3. At some stage during this time, wash and finely chop the mint leaves and mix with the mayonnaise.
4. After 1 of those 2 hours of the chicken swimming in the ginger beer, light the fire and once the coals are ready an hour later, braai the meat.
5. Braai the meat for about 6–10 minutes on hot coals until it is done. The nice thing about chicken breast fillets is that you can actually see the meat colour changing from raw to ready on the braai. Take the meat off the fire when ready.
6. Butter or oil the sliced bread and toast on the grid, taking care not to over-toast (burn) them. I serve the Mule open, and as such use a slice of bread as opposed to a roll but a roll will work just as fine.
7. Assemble the burger: Buttered and toasted bread, lettuce, tomato, chicken breast, minted mayonnaise.
8. It is important to serve the Mule with a slice of lemon so as to have all the classic ingredients of the namesake cocktail present on the plate. Bonus points if you sear the lemon on the fire.

AND ...

If you serve the meal with glasses of vodka, this is a Moscow Mule and if you serve it with tequila, it's a Mexican Mule. If, on the other hand, you wash it down with brandy, it's not a mule at all – we then call it by its South African name: the Karoo Donkie.

SMOG BURGER

Pizza fans will appreciate that this burger is quite clearly inspired by the SMOG pizza: salami, mushroom, onion and green pepper. It's a globally popular flavour combination for wood-fired pizzas and here we're adapting it for the South African braai fire. Combine the four with some braaied chicken breasts and fresh fire-toasted rolls and you have yourself a winner!

WHAT YOU NEED
(makes 4)

4 chicken breast fillets
4 hamburger rolls
olive oil
salt and freshly ground pepper
1 onion (sliced)
2 green peppers (sliced)
1 punnet (250 g) **mushrooms** (sliced)
2 garlic cloves (crushed and chopped)
8–12 slices salami
120 g Cheddar cheese (sliced or grated)

WHAT TO DO

1. Pack the chicken breast fillets on a chopping board and cover with cling wrap. Now pound the thick side of each piece of meat with a meat mallet, wine bottle, rolling pin, side of a meat cleaver or any other item of sufficient weight and size. You want the meat to relax so that the whole fillet is more uniform in thickness. This step will make the meat easier to braai, better-looking on your burger and more tender to bite. While the cling wrap will not aid in any of these goals, nor influence the final taste of the burger, it will prevent small pieces of chicken meat flying all over the place. If you're trying to use less plastic in your house and don't have cling wrap, don't perform this step inside the kitchen. Go and stand in the garden where small pieces of chicken meat can freely roam!

2. Give each chicken fillet a light coating of olive oil. Either brush each fillet with oil or pour a bit of oil onto them and toss them around until they are all coated. Also season the meat with salt and pepper or your favourite braai salt.

3. Make the sauce by heating some olive oil in a potjie or fireproof pan, then add the onion and green pepper. Sauté for a few minutes until it starts to get a nice colour, and then add the mushrooms and garlic. Now toss and fry the whole lot until you like the look of it. Season to taste with salt and pepper.

4. Braai the meat for about 6–10 minutes on hot coals until it is done. The nice thing about chicken breast fillets is that you can actually see the meat colour changing from raw to ready on the braai. When you are satisfied that the chicken is almost ready and you've turned it for a final time, distribute the Cheddar cheese onto the chicken breasts. You want the heat from the meat and fire to melt the cheese slightly. Now you can't turn the chicken again, as the cheese will be lost to the coals. Take the meat off the fire when ready.

5. Oil the sliced rolls and toast on the grid, taking care not to over-toast (burn) them.

6. Assemble the burger: Roll, slices of salami, braaied chicken fillets with cheese, onion, pepper and mushroom sauce, roll.

AND …

This flavour combination also works very well when you replace the chicken with a homemade 100% pure-beef patty.

CHICKEN, FETA AND SUN-DRIED TOMATO BURGER

All burger patties are not created equal. As far as chicken goes, this one is pretty regal.

WHAT YOU NEED
(makes 4)

4 chicken breast fillets
4 hamburger rolls
1 pack (200–250 g) **sun-dried tomatoes**
2 feta cheese rounds
salt and pepper
olive oil
fresh basil or rocket leaves
tinfoil

WHAT TO DO

1. Drain the sun-dried tomatoes and keep their marinade or brine for the last step when you will dress the burgers with it.
2. Dice the chicken breasts, feta and sun-dried tomatoes into pieces. Mix them together in a bowl with salt and pepper and a little olive oil – just enough oil to make the mixture stick together.
3. Divide the mixture into four, and make four patties using your recently washed hands or a patty press.
4. Place a sheet of tinfoil in a hinged grid, and grease the foil in four patches with olive oil. Place the patties on these four spots and start to braai. The risk of burning is minimal due to the foil, so heat is not your enemy and you can braai on hot-to-very-hot coals.
5. Place another sheet of oiled foil on top of the patties, close the grid, and turn. Continue braaing the patties between the sheets of foil until the patties are firm. Remove the foil and braai once more on each side to brown the patties.
6. Oil the insides of the cut rolls and toast on the grid, taking care not to over-toast (burn) them.
7. Assemble the burger: Roll, basil or rocket leaves, patty; then dress with sun-dried tomato sauce from step 1 and close the roll.

AND ...

This recipe is inspired by Lise Beyers, one of the first journalists to support National Braai Day in print (i.e. I like her). She uses pitted black olives instead of sun-dried tomato, doesn't tell you to include the fresh leaves on the burger and braais the patties without the aid of tinfoil. I suggest you try all these options and see what works for you.

BLUE CHEESE BURGER

The pungent taste of blue cheese released by the heat of a braaied chicken breast fillet combines expertly with the sweetness and texture of preserved green figs to create a truly memorable braai-eating experience. But there are a few other reasons I think that this is a really good recipe. The shopping list is very short and all the ingredients can be obtained quite easily on a quick jog through a supermarket. Then, once you get home or to the picnic or campsite, the only thing you need to do is light the fire. Once the coals are ready, and with absolutely no other preparation, you can quite easily make these burgers in under 10 minutes. Everything that needs to be done can be done while the chicken is on the braai. Last but not least, the burgers are very photogenic. It is an indisputable fact that good-looking food tastes even better.

WHAT YOU NEED
(makes 4)

4 chicken breast fillets
4 hamburger rolls
olive oil
salt and pepper
butter lettuce (the type with attitude, or even rocket leaves)
1 block (250 g) **blue cheese** (sliced or crumbled)
4–8 preserved green figs (sliced)

WHAT TO DO

1. Pack the chicken breast fillets on a chopping board and cover with cling wrap. Now pound the thick side of each piece of meat with a meat mallet, wine bottle, rolling pin, side of a meat cleaver or any other item of sufficient weight and size. You want the meat to relax so that the whole fillet is more uniform in thickness. This step will make the meat easier to braai, better-looking on your burger and more tender to bite. While the cling wrap will not aid in any of these goals, nor influence the final taste of the burger, it will prevent small pieces of chicken meat flying all over the place. If you're trying to use less plastic in your house and don't have cling wrap, don't perform this step inside the kitchen. Go and stand in the garden where small pieces of chicken meat can freely roam!
2. Give each chicken fillet a light coating of olive oil. Either brush each fillet with oil or pour a bit of oil onto them and toss them around until they are all coated. Also season the meat with salt and pepper or your favourite braai salt.
3. Braai the chicken for about 6–10 minutes on hot coals until it is done. The nice thing about chicken breast fillets is that you can actually see the meat colour changing from raw to ready on the braai. Take the meat off the fire when ready.
4. Oil the sliced rolls and toast on the grid, taking care not to over-toast (burn) them.
5. Assemble the burger: Roll, lettuce, chicken breast, sliced or crumbled blue cheese, slices of preserved green figs, roll.

AND ...

When assembling burgers I always like to place the cheese right next to the patty so that the heat of the meat can melt the cheese slightly and release some flavours.

KLEIN KAROO CHICKEN BURGER

This one started out while on holiday in an ancient and massive villa, almost but not quite a castle, on a hilltop overlooking the countryside of Umbria in Italy. On that occasion, the sauce was served with veal but back home, the sauce found its true home on chicken. We call it the Klein Karoo Chicken Burger because of the strong agricultural association that the beautiful part of South Africa has with some of the core ingredients; namely, olives, wine, and when it's in season, bright-red sun-ripened tomatoes. The fact that the Klein Karoo in South Africa gives Umbria in Italy a run for its money in terms of climate and natural beauty also doesn't hurt.

WHAT YOU NEED
(makes 4)

4 chicken breast fillets
4 hamburger rolls
1 lemon (or 2 small lemons or limes)
olive oil
salt and pepper
1 onion (chopped)
4 garlic cloves (crushed and chopped)
1 cup olives (pitted and roughly chopped)
1 tot capers
1 pack/tub (in oil or water, 200–300 g) **sun-dried tomatoes**
1 cup white wine
200 g feta cheese (optional)
2 tomatoes (sliced)
fresh basil leaves

WHAT TO DO

1. Place the chicken breast fillets on a chopping board and cover with cling wrap. Now pound the thick side of each piece of meat with a meat mallet, wine bottle, rolling pin, side of a meat cleaver or any other item of sufficient weight and size. You want the meat to relax so that the whole fillet is more uniform in thickness. This step will make the meat easier to braai, better-looking on your burger and more tender to bite. While the cling wrap will not aid in any of these goals, nor influence the final taste of the burger, it will prevent small pieces of chicken meat flying all over the place. If you're trying to use less plastic in your house and don't have cling wrap, don't perform this step inside the kitchen. Go and stand in the garden where small pieces of chicken meat can freely roam!

2. Squeeze lemon juice over the chicken fillets and let that soak in for a few minutes (a few weeks would be too long). Now give each chicken fillet a light coating of olive oil. Either brush each fillet with oil or pour a bit of oil onto them and toss them around until they are all coated. Also season the meat with salt and pepper or your favourite braai salt.

3. While you wait for the fire, chop the onion and garlic, and remove the pits from the olives. Drain the capers.

4. When the coals are almost ready to braai the chicken, start to make the sauce. Place a fireproof pot or pan over the heat and sauté the chopped onion in oil for a few minutes. When the onion has colour, add the garlic, olives, sun-dried tomatoes plus their sauce, and the drained capers. Regularly toss this mixture with your wooden spoon until it is well combined and starts to 'fry'. You do not need to add any salt as the sauce will contain enough of it via the capers and olives.

5. Add the white wine, stir and then let the sauce gently simmer, stirring now and again so that the wine can reduce by half in the time it takes you to braai the chicken.

6. Braai the meat for about 6–10 minutes on hot coals until it is done. The nice thing about chicken breast fillets is that you can actually see the meat colour changing from raw to ready on the braai. Take the meat off the fire when ready.

7. Oil the insides of the cut rolls and toast on the grid, taking care not to over-toast (burn) them.

8. Assemble the burger: Roll, tomato, chicken, sauce, feta cheese (optional), basil, roll.

CHICKEN CAESAR BURGER

For many years the Caesar has been one of the world's classic salads. But as a chicken burger on the braai, we are giving this flavour combination the chance to reach its full potential. Firstly, a braaied chicken breast fillet is superior to any other version of that meat, and secondly, a roll toasted on the coals of a wood fire is clearly going to trump any crouton prepared in a kitchen. The sauce is very easy to make in a pestle and mortar, food processor or stick blender. If you still don't have any of these essential pieces of culinary equipment, buy at least one now. You will use it to work the garlic, capers and anchovy fillets into a smooth paste, which forms the cornerstone of the sauce's flavour. As with most other recipes in this book, I am truly excited to introduce you to this one, as it is really good.

WHAT YOU NEED
(makes 4)

4 chicken breast fillets
4 hamburger rolls
olive oil
salt and pepper
2 garlic cloves
3 anchovy fillets
1 tsp capers (drained)
½ cup mayonnaise (creamy)
1 tsp mustard
1 tsp Worcestershire sauce
1 head romaine lettuce (also known as cos lettuce, torn apart and washed – if you can't find one, use standard lettuce)
3 tots Parmesan cheese (grated or shaved)

WHAT TO DO

1. Pack the chicken breast fillets on a chopping board and cover with cling wrap. Now pound the thick side of each piece of meat with a meat mallet, wine bottle, rolling pin, side of a meat cleaver or any other item of sufficient weight and size. You want the meat to relax so that the whole fillet is more uniform in thickness. This step will make the meat easier to braai, better-looking on your burger and more tender to bite. While the cling wrap will not aid in any of these goals, nor influence the final taste of the burger, it will prevent small pieces of chicken meat flying all over the place. If you're trying to use less plastic in your house and don't have cling wrap, don't perform this step inside the kitchen. Go and stand in the garden where small pieces of chicken meat can freely roam!
2. Give each chicken fillet a light coating of olive oil. Either brush each fillet with oil or pour a bit of oil onto them and toss them around until they are all coated. Also season the meat with salt and pepper or your favourite braai salt.
3. Make the sauce: Put the garlic, anchovies and capers in your pestle and mortar, food processor or stick blender and grind/blend into a smooth paste. Now add the mayonnaise, mustard and Worcestershire sauce. Mix well until everything is properly combined.
4. Braai the meat for about 6–10 minutes on hot coals until it is done. The nice thing about chicken breast fillets is that you can actually see the meat colour changing from raw to ready on the braai. Take the meat off the fire when ready.
5. Oil the sliced rolls and toast on the grid, taking care not to over-toast (burn) them.
6. Assemble the burger: Roll, lettuce, braaied chicken breast, sauce, Parmesan, roll.

OTHER GREAT BOOKS FROM JAN BRAAI:

- Fireworks
- Red Hot
- The Democratic Republic of Braai
- Shisanyama
- The Vegetarian Option

Available in both English and Afrikaans

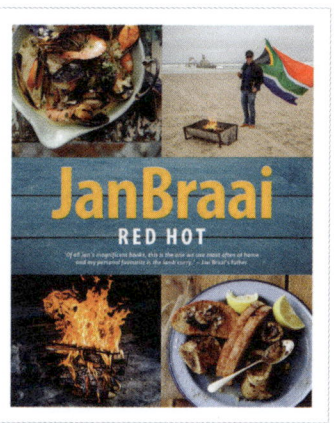

Text © Jan Braai 2020
Photographs © Jan Braai 2020

All rights reserved. No part of this book may be reproduced or transmitted in any form or by any means, electronic or mechanical, including photocopying, recording or any information storage or retrieval system, without permission from the copyright holder.

ISBN: 978-1-928257-82-0
e-ISBN: 978-1-928257-83-7

First published by Bookstorm in 2020
Reprinted 2022

Published by Bookstorm (Pty) Ltd
PO Box 4532
Northcliff 2115
Johannesburg
South Africa
www.bookstorm.co.za

Edited by Kelly Norwood-Young
Proofread by Salome Posthumus
Food styling by Christien Durand, Brita du Plessis
Photography by Guillaume Bosch, Matthys van Lill
Cover design by Guillaume Bosch, Wilna Combrinck
Typography by mr design
Printed by ABC Press, Cape Town

INDEX

Anchovy 64, 196
   Anchovy, caper and olive braaibroodjie 64
Apple tart braaibroodjie 94

Bacon 29, 32, 46, 58, 120, 134, 138, 148, 184
   Bacon and banana braaibroodjie 29
   Bacon and cheese burger, Spiced 148
   Bacon burger, Cheese and 120
   Bacon, pineapple and sweet-chilli burger 134
Bagel braaibroodjie 74
Banana braaibroodjie, Bacon and 29
Bash burger, The 136
Beef 34, 76, 80, 103, 104, 107, 108, 110, 112, 114, 117, 118, 120, 122, 124, 127, 130, 133, 134, 136, 138, 141, 142, 146, 148, 150
Beer burger, The stout 122
Best amazing mushroom burger, The 103
Big burger, The 118
Biltong braaibroodjie 22
Blue cheese 43, 192
   Blue cheese burger 192
Bobotie burger 110
Boerewors 159, 162
   Boerewors sliders, Sherry 162
Bolognese quesadillas 80
Bone marrow burger, Fillet and 108
Braai Freedom Fighter 130
Braaibroodjies 18-97
Braaied butternut braaibroodjie 68
Bread 10-12, 16, 176
Break-time braaibroodjie 41
Breakfast braaibroodjie 32
Brie 146
Burger braaibroodjie, The 76
Burgers 100-196
Burgundy burger 146
Butternut braaibroodjie, Braaied 68

Calamari braaibroodjie 62
Camembert 146, 182
   Camembert, fig and bacon burger, Chicken 182
Cape Malay fish burger 172
Caper burger, Mustard and 128
Caprese burger 104
Caramel braaibroodjie 87
Chakalaka burger 145
Cheese and bacon burger 120
Cheese and herb braaibroodjie 50
Cheese burger, Spiced bacon and 148

Cheese burgers 103, 104, 114, 118, 120, 134, 136, 138, 142, 146, 148, 150, 154, 164, 166, 166, 172, 178, 180, 182, 184, 188, 190, 192, 194, 196
Chicken
   Braaibroodjies 46, 48, 52
   Burgers 17, 178, 180, 182, 184, 186, 188, 190, 192, 194, 196
   Chicken burger, Crispy 180
   Chicken burger, Klein Karoo 194
   Chicken Caesar burger 196
   Chicken liver braaibroodjie, Peri-peri 48
   Chicken mayo braaibroodjie 52
   Chicken prego roll 178
   Chicken, Camembert, fig and bacon burger 182
   Chicken, feta and sun-dried tomato burger 190
Chimichurri steak roll 133
Chocolate braaibroodjie 90
Chocolate braaibroodjie, Marshmallow and 96
Choripán burger 159
Chorizo braaibroodjie 26
Classic scone braaibroodjie 88
Club braaibroodjie 46
Cream cheese 22, 50, 55, 64, 74, 84
Crispy chicken burger 180
Curry mince braaibroodjie 34

Deluxe braaibroodjie 58
Dessert 87, 90, 92, 94, 96

Eggs 32, 110
Empanada braaibroodjie 56

Feta and sun-dried tomato burger, Chicken 190
Feta 24, 30, 36, 60, 152, 166, 172, 184, 190, 194
Figs 60, 182, 192
   Fig and bacon burger, Chicken, Camembert 182
   Fig and feta braaibroodjie 60
Fillet and bone marrow burger 108
Fish
   Braaibroodjies see Seafood braaibroodjies
   Fish burger, Cape Malay 172
   Fish burgers see Seafood burgers
   Fish cake burger 171

Garlic burger, The 142
Greek-style braaibroodjie 36

Hake 172
Ham 58, 70
Hamburger

History of 12
   Patties 14
Hand-chopped burger 127
Holy Trinity braaibroodjie 39

Iced-tea sandwich, The 84
Irish Wild West Coast burger 138

Jan Braai lamb pita 78
Jan Braai pizza 83

Klein Karoo chicken burger 194
Klein Karoo ostrich burger 164

Lamb 78, 152
   Lamb burger 152
   Lamb pita, Jan Braai 78

Macaroni and cheese braaibroodjie 72
Madagascan peppercorn burger 112
Marshmallow and chocolate braaibroodjie 96
Mince braaibroodjie, Curry 34
Monkeygland burger 107
Mozzarella 43, 44, 60, 104, 134, 184
Mule, The 186
Mushrooms 55, 83, 103 122, 166, 188
   Mushroom braaibroodjie 55
   Mushroom burger, The best amazing 103
   Mushroom burger, The Revolutionary 166
Mustard and caper burger 128

Nacho burger 114

Ostrich burger, Klein Karoo 164

Parmesan 196
Patties, hamburger 14-16
Peppercorn burger, Madagascan 112
Peri-peri chicken liver braaibroodjie 48
Pineapple and sweet-chilli burger, Bacon 134
Pizza, Jan Braai 83
Pork 154, 156, 159, 160
   Pork belly burger 156
   Pork neck burger 154
   Pork party, Pulled 160
Potato wedges 174
Prego roll, Chicken 178
Prego roll, Steak 117
Pulled pork party 160

Quesadillas, Bolognaise 80

Raclette braaibroodjie 70
Revolutionary mushroom burger, The 166
Rogan Josh burger 141
Roosterkoek 176
Rotherhamburger, The 184
Rump steak 112, 117, 124, 127, 133

Sauce
   Burger 127, 136
   Chakalaka 145
   Chimichurri 133, 159
   Garlic 142
   Monkeygland 107
   Mushroom 103
   Mustard 128
   Peppercorn, Madagascan 112
   Pesto 104
   Prego 117, 178
   Ranch 160
   Rogan Josh 141
   Tzatziki 152
   Yoghurt 78
Scone braaibroodjie, Classic 88
Seafood
   Braaibroodjies 62, 64, 67, 74
   Burgers 168, 171, 172, 196
Sherry boerewors sliders 162
Sirloin steak 117, 124, 127, 133
Sloppy Jan 150
SMOG burger 188
Snoek braaibroodjie 67
Spanakopita braaibroodjie 30
Spiced bacon and cheese burger 148
Steak 112, 117, 124, 127, 133
   Rump 112, 117, 124, 127, 133
   Sirloin 117, 124, 127, 133
   Steak prego roll 117
   Steak roll, Chimichurri 133
   Steak sandwich with mustard, mayo and caramelised onions 124
Stout beer burger, The 122
Sun-dried tomato burger, Chicken, Feta and 190
Supermodel, The 24
Sweet-chilli burger, Bacon and pineapple 134

Teriyaki tuna burger 168
Three-cheese braaibroodjie 43
Tortilla 80
Traditional braaibroodjie 20
Tuna burger, Teriyaki 168

Vegetarian
   Braaibroodjies 20, 24, 30, 36, 39, 41, 43, 50, 55, 56, 68, 72, 83, 84, 87, 88, 90, 92, 94, 96
   Burger 166
   Sides 174, 176

Waffle braaibroodjie 92
West Coast braaibroodjie 44